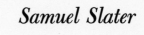

Samuel Slater

SAMUEL SLATER

Father of

American Manufactures

by

E. H. CAMERON

American Saga
SERIES

THE BOND WHEELWRIGHT COMPANY

H. N. Slater, great-grandson of Samuel Slater, has made the production of this book possible by his inspiring counsel, supported by numerous documents pertaining to his famous forebear that he has made available. His sponsorship of this biography represents one indication, only, of his determined effort to consolidate and amplify the historical story of the tremendous part played by Samuel Slater in the early growth of American industry. Such efforts have continued for a third of a century. They include his part in the founding of the Old Slater Mill Association, his driving energy that led to the initiation of the Old Slater Mill Museum, and his endowment to the Massachusetts Institute of Technology of the Slater Memorial Laboratory, noted for its research on modern textile processes.

H. Nelson Slater has contributed advice and, upon many occasions, financial assistance to these agencies that they might continue to stand as memorials of his brilliant ancestor, Samuel Slater.

FOREWORD

IN THE EARLY DAYS of American independence, this country
was largely agricultural, and it was in the interest of England
that it should remain so. The recent inventions of machinery
and skill in factory management had given England a mono-
poly in manufactured goods. As the British wished to export
their goods, they forbade the export of machinery and the
emigration of mechanics. For this reason, Samuel Slater left
England for America as a farmer, taking with him only his
indenture which proved his familiarity with the spinning of
cotton at the mill of Jedediah Strutt in Belper.

Upon arriving in New York after a sixty-six-day voyage
from London, Slater soon discovered that there was little
prospect of finding in this area the cotton manufacturing facilities that he sought. However, by good fortune, he was
directed by a Captain Brown, whom he met in New York, to
Moses Brown, of Providence, to whom he wrote a letter out-
lining his experience with Strutt and Arkwright. To this letter
Moses Brown promptly replied with an invitation to call on
him in Providence. Shortly after this meeting, an agreement
was entered into between them, which started Slater's employment by Brown, to duplicate the Arkwright machinery at a
wage of one dollar per day. From this small beginning the
American industrial system was created.

From then on, Samuel Slater's career was one of continual expansion, as he built and managed cotton mills in Rhode Island, Connecticut, Massachusetts, and New Hampshire, alone and with various partners.

The factory methods introduced by Slater greatly influenced the economic growth of the country. Many people found employment in his mills and many more in other mills which sprang up as a result of this great textile pioneer's success. His fame was such that President Jackson called on Slater in the spring of 1833 in order to meet the man who was responsible for the tremendous development of the American textile industry, and thereupon named him "The Father of American Manufactures."

ACKNOWLEDGMENTS

Despite the strong emphasis of historians on the major part played by Samuel Slater in the early development of American industry, biographical literature on Slater is scant. The prime source of information is the *Memoir of Samuel Slater*, written shortly after his death by his friend, George S. White. This book is replete with lengthy dissertations on the most important problem of the young United States of America—its paucity of manufacturing facilities—and it is quoted by historians on this subject. Interspersed with such data are those on Samuel Slater, limited in scope and lacking a complete chronological account of his career.

The White biography, however, draws upon its author's personal acquaintance with Slater and is thus a contemporary account of his career. As such it is invaluable, as far as it goes.

Reference to the Bibliography of the present book will indicate its other textual sources on Samuel Slater.

Dr. Frederick L. Lewton, former Curator of Textiles, United States National Museum, made an extensive study of the career of Samuel Slater during the 1940's, upon which his unpublished *Biography of Samuel Slater* is based. Dr. Lewton carried on a notable project of research on the subject—exhaustive, accurate, and logically presented. The present biographer has drawn heavily on his manuscript.

When the present Mr. Slater sent a copy of Dr. Lewton's manuscript to an old friend for a report, however, he told Mr. Slater that the biography of Samuel Slater had still to be written.

Thereupon the younger Slater called upon Mr. M. D. C. Crawford for help. Crawford had written *The Heritage of Cotton* in 1924, and revised it in 1948 for the Fairfield Publishing Company of New York. At Mr. Slater's request he wrote the *Samuel Slater Story* as a pamphlet for the Old Slater Mill Association in 1948, the purpose of which was to solicit contributions toward the endowment fund of the Association, of which Mr. Slater was the chairman. With these funds, the trustees were able to establish the old Slater Mill as a textile museum.

However, Crawford died, in July 1949, before he could complete a biography.

We are particularly indebted to the late Daniel Tower, first Curator of the Old Slater Mill Museum, whose comprehensive notes on Slater were made available. These include his study of the Almy & Brown papers at the Rhode Island Historical Society, similar studies of the Old Slater Mill, and notes on obscure details of the early Arkwright models, the Crompton mule, and certain patent matters. Such points were given us to check in English museums.

Others versed in the knowledge of early textile history to whom our thanks are due are: Messrs. Taylor and Watkins, and Miss Grace Rogers, at Smithsonian; Mr. George West, for his analysis of the first Slater Mill equipment; those of

Slatersville and Webster who gave information on various Slater matters at these locations; Mr. R. W. Lovett and Professor G. S. Gibb of the Baker Library, who made available portions of the extensive collection of documents of Slater mills; and Professor Herbert Heaton, University of Minnesota, for his account of old English immigration procedures.

Those in England to whom we are indebted for data on the English period of Slater are: Mr. C. E. Harrison, Managing Director of the English Sewing Cotton Company, Ltd.; Mr. H. D. Ryde, Manager of the Belper Mills; Professor R. S. Fitton, author of a history of W. G. & J. Strutt; Mr. K. R. Gilbert, of the Science Museum, London; Professor C. S. Ashton of the London School of Economics; Mr. Ernest Bletcher, Librarian, County Borough of Derby; Miss G. E. Allen, Principal of the Matlock Training College for Women; and Mr. H. H. Clinch of the Platt Brothers Museum in Oldham.

Contents

ILLUSTRATIONS

SAMUEL SLATER

►

INTRODUCTION

IN THE ANNALS of American textile history the career of Samuel Slater is treated with a respect bordering on reverence, because of his outstanding contribution to the success of the early textile industry in the United States.* A review of the textile arts from their primitive beginnings is necessary to appreciate fully this tribute to one of the great pioneer industrialists of America. Such a review emphasizes the accomplishments of Slater and others of his generation who introduced the machine processes by which modern mankind is properly clothed. However much we may marvel at the handicraft skills of our ancestors that the records of the past reveal, we have to realize their complete inadequacy to supply the demands of today.

When archeologists excavated certain areas of the prehistoric Lake Dwellers' region in Alpine Switzerland and Northern Italy, they found evidences of an early textile culture. They found crude but serviceable fabrics of bast (the fibrous inner bark of trees), flax and wool, as well as flax in bales, ready for the spinners. Their further discoveries gave authentic evidence that primitive methods of spinning and weaving were practiced in the earliest era of the Stone Age.

---

* *See* Note 1, Appendix A, p. 179.

Evidence of similar prehistoric textile industries has been unearthed in many parts of the world, and some authorities believe that the genesis of the arts of spinning and weaving was contemporaneous with the discovery of fire for cooking and the building of the earliest forms of shelter. This hypothesis appears logical, for food, shelter, and raiment were prime requisites of our primitive ancestors. They were basic necessities of living, as indeed they are today. Leaving the period of prehistoric time, for which our knowledge of the past has to depend on the relics discovered by archeologists, such as those found in the Lake Dwellers' region, we come to the period of ancient history when men began to make records of the activities of their day, for future generations to read.

In the period of ancient history, the Bible, the writings of Homer and Confucius, besides many hieroglyphics, make references to spinning and weaving. These show that the Chinese, Hindus, Assyrians, Babylonians, Persians, Egyptians, and Hebrews had spun yarn and made it into cloth since very remote times. Similar records or relics reveal the textile skills of the ancient Peruvians and Mexicans and the Indians of the Americas.

Although the products of the time of ancient history were far superior to those made in prehistoric times, they were limited in amount and in quality by the handicraft methods used, which required talented men and women to perform them. Some of their products were excellent, but obtainable only by those of great wealth. We may be certain that it was a very rich Egyptian whose mummy is clothed in linen cloth containing five hundred and forty warp threads to the inch— a fineness that modern textile mills would have to take special

2

measures to produce. The ancient pagans therefore rated the textile arts very highly, and credited the proficiency of their spinners and weavers to the deities whom they worshipped. Ancient statues show the Egyptian goddess Isis holding a shuttle, for they believed that she had invented the art of weaving. The Assyrians claimed this accomplishment for their own Queen Semiramis. The ancient Greeks portrayed their goddess Minerva with a distaff; in their belief, she had taught mankind how to spin. Not of celestial rank, yet highly regarded by the Greeks, was Penelope, the heroine of Homer's *Odyssey*, for she was their symbol of the art of weaving.

Following the Dark Ages, the handicraft textile arts kept pace, as civilization continued its advance from East to West, when spinning and weaving were extended to Italy and Greece, thence to Spain, France, Flanders, and Germany and thence to England. William the Conqueror, who invaded England (A.D. 1066), found that the Angles and the Saxons could spin and weave with considerable skill.

Most notable in the textile art in the European countries were the Flemish. Following the Norman Conquest, many Flemish weavers emigrated to England, settling in the western section, now Lancashire. The Lancashire area ultimately became the center of the great handicraft textile industry of England, where yarn and cloth of satisfactory quality were produced by hand methods for many generations, up to the beginning of the Industrial Revolution two hundred years ago.

Thus we can see that among our forebears who lived in Europe and Great Britain two centuries ago, there were many craftsmen skilled in the textile arts. They made fine raiment for the wealthy, and clothing less splendid but of stout wearing quality, for the common people of the regions in which they lived. Their handmade creations were often of superior quality, comparable to that now produced by machine. A pleasant aura of romance surrounds the old high spinning wheels, treadle wheels, and hand looms of two centuries ago, for as we have seen, such hand equipment dates back to the dawn of history, with few changes since the days of ancient Egypt, Assyria, and Greece.

The primitive hand spindle, which was a simple stick of wood with a cleft end, had been improved by the addition of the whorl, a doughnut shaped member of bone, baked clay, or stone, which was slipped over the spindle's larger end. It gave momentum to the revolving spindle as it was whirled through the air by the spinner. The tangled mass of fibres was wound on the distaff, or "rock," from which the spinner would draw out and align the fibres into a strand with one hand as he spun it into yarn on the spindle manipulated by his other hand. After long centuries these crude devices gave way to the high, or "walking wheel" spinner, and this to the "low" treadle wheel of our forefathers in the period preceding the American Revolution, and the hand loom was still the only device for weaving at this time.

The hand-operated textile equipment of two centuries ago could not begin to supply the modern demand for yarn and fabric. The tremendous productive capacity of our modern textile mills stems from the remarkable evolution of textile machine processes developed in the Industrial Revolution in England (1760-1830).

During the time the American Colonies were fighting for their freedom in the Revolutionary War, the textile-machine

4

methods of the Industrial Revolution in England were being developed with rapid strides. Six years after the end of the Revolution, in the year 1789, the success of machine methods in England had become spectacular. These factory methods were made to order for the industrially impoverished United States of America, which became a sovereign nation in this year with the adoption of our Constitution.

Two types of genius, rarely possessed by any one individual concurrently, were essential to the success of the machine methods of the Industrial Revolution. The first was the inventive talent of those who conceived these unique machines. The second was that of the industrialists who could make the crude machines work and produce yarn and fabric at such high profits that investors were induced to finance the novel cotton mills.

Jedediah Strutt was one of these rare individuals, one of the most distinguished of the early textile industrialists in England, noted for the inventive skill and business ability exhibited in his operation of some of the earliest mills for the machine spinning of cotton yarn. Under this good master, Samuel Slater served as an apprentice for more than six years. Upon completing his term with Strutt, Slater came to America in the year 1789 and introduced the machine methods of cotton spinning here a year later.

Slater was then a youth of twenty-two. When he died, nearly half a century later, he had not only proved the merits of machine methods in his own extensive operations, but had trained many other men in their intricacies and caused still others to start textile ventures of their own, inspired by his success. He had found America dependent upon textile handicraft methods that had been used with little change since the days of the ancient Greeks and Romans. At the time of his death the population of the United States had increased fourfold and the machines of the thriving textile industry of his adopted country were providing vast quantities of good quality raiment for these Americans at low cost. So great was the part played by Slater in this dramatic advance that Andrew Jackson, then President of the United States, correctly expressed the sentiment of many American citizens of his generation when he called Samuel Slater "the father of American manufactures."

I
Apprenticeship
1768-1789

1

WHEN HE WAS A little boy and had time to play, Samuel Slater would enjoy the River Derwent. It offered so many attractions to a normal boy who was fortunate enough to live near such a lively stream and liked to swim, fish, and sail. When he became a serious-minded youngster of fourteen and began to think of going to work, he was to find that the river was a powerful worker itself. Even an apprentice could appreciate this, as he watched it turn the cumbrous wooden water wheel that served the cotton mill of the great Jedediah Strutt.

The River Derwent flows southeasterly from its source in the High Peak Country to its mouth at the River Trent, splitting the County of Derbyshire into two parts. As smaller streams join the Derwent in its upper sections, the volume of its flow is increased, causing its current to run swiftly as it winds between the limestone crags along its course to the south.

Before the day of the steam engine, the swift flow and ample volume of the River Derwent provided a prime source of power for the hamlets, villages, and townships along the shores of its lower reaches—a power vastly more potent than that of the muscles of men and beasts. On the Derwent, the world's first spinning mill to be driven by water power was built at Cromford, in the year 1771, and other mills were soon erected on it, at Matlock, Matlock Bath, Belper, Milford, and Derby.

The little River Derwent thus played an active part in the dramatic change in the textile methods which took place during the Industrial Revolution in England. It also played an important part in the early career of Samuel Slater.

In the year 1782, a successful entrepreneur in the new industry was Jedediah Strutt of Belper, who was expanding his promising ventures and needed more mill hands to work for him. When he asked his friend William Slater, who lived close to Belper, to let him have his oldest son as an apprentice, Slater, sure that this son wanted to become a farmer, recommended a younger son, Samuel, instead. "He writes well and is good at figures," he explained. The acceptance of his friend's advice resulted in Strutt's playing a dual role during the next few years. Not only did he extend his operations in the machine spinning of cotton yarn—which made him a major figure in textile history—but he also trained in the new methods the youth who later played the leading part in the introduction of these methods which were major factors in the Industrial Revolution in America. Both master and apprentice became outstanding characters in the remarkable drama of the change from the domestic system of textile manufacture to the factory system—Strutt in his own country, England, and Slater in the land of his adoption, America.

William Slater was a Derbyshire farmer, in the class of yeoman: a designation that meant that his ancestors back to feudal times had held certain rights of independence that even the King of England could not deny. The various conquerors of England—the Romans, Norsemen, and Normans—treated Derbyshire men with high respect; they were a belligerent people, and not to be trifled with. William had increased his

10

holdings by the purchase of lands for their timber, thus becoming a timber merchant as well as a farmer. He was noted for his integrity and ability.

William had inherited the paternal Slater domicile, Holly House, near Belper Township, Derbyshire County. The newspaper account of his death describes him as "Mr. William Slater, (a wealthy Farmer of Black-Brook near Duffield)." Actually Black-Brook might better have been called a suburb of Belper, which township is now generally considered as the place of Samuel Slater's birth and is located in the southern section of Derbyshire County. Like many Derbyshire homes, Holly House was located on a hill. (The steep road leading to it is called Longwalls Lane at the present time, because of the sturdy and straight gritstone walls that bound it.) Holly House was also built of gritstone—two stories high, with a straw-thatched roof. It adjoined a long stone stable and was surrounded by cultivated fields and pastures, separated by tall hedgerows and also stone walls, for stone is plentiful in the rugged terrain of southern Derbyshire.

Holly House is now in ruins and one must depend upon descriptions of the farmhouses of the period to draw a picture of its interior. It had ground floors of smooth limestone, and the upper floors were of roughly-planed boards, supported by floor beams adzed from the trunks of small trees. The house was heated by fireplaces, the one in the kitchen having an oven at one end and on the other, iron hooks from which were usually hung sides of bacon being smoked to a pleasant savor. There was a tall settle or two, and high-back chairs, and an oak dresser mounted with pewter dishes and tankards in one or another of the rooms of the house.

11

Throughout the house the rhythmic clatter of loom and smooth whir of spinning wheel announced that warm clothing for the family was under preparation, made from the clean wool of sheep that William Slater reared.

Holly House was thus well-furnished, in keeping with the standing of the prosperous farmer of the Derbyshire of two hundred years ago. Here William Slater took his bride, Elizabeth Fox, and here they brought up their large family. Their children were baptized in ancient Duffield Church, near Belper, built on the site of a previous church that appears to have existed before the Norman Conquest. The register of Duffield Church states that Samuel Slater, their fifth child and second son, was baptized "4th July, 1768," about a month after his birth on June 9.

In keeping with his position, William Slater gave Samuel a good education. At the school of Master Thomas Jackson he learned to write a good hand, as evidenced by his signature to his indenture to Jedediah Strutt, whose own signature to this famous document is a little hard to decipher. Master Jackson also taught Samuel a clear, logical, and forceful style of English composition, so well recorded in later family and business letters. Attesting to the religious upbringing of Samuel Slater are the frequent Biblical references which his adult correspondence contains.

There were always boy-chores for Samuel to do—long rows of garden stuff to weed, sheep to help tend, wood boxes to keep filled during the winter months, hens' eggs to gather from the pungent nests, and even the winding of the yarn, spun by his mother on her spinning wheel. Like all well-brought-up Derbyshire farm boys, he learned early in life that while play

12

was proper for a normal boy, his education and the performance of his share of the work came first.

Samuel excelled in arithmetic, which pleased Master Jackson, who said that scholars well versed in duodecimals and
vulgar fractions usually made good businessmen in later life.
As a boy, Samuel gave early signs of his mechanical skill when
he made a polished steel spindle to facilitate his chore of winding worsted for his mother. He grew up to be a healthy
youngster, resembling his father in his ruddy complexion and
strong physique.

When he was approaching the age of fourteen, at the time
of Strutt's request for an apprentice, Samuel was called upon
to play a man's part during a family crisis—a tragic accident
to his father.

Because of William Slater's experience in the purchase of
local real estate, it was natural that Jedediah Strutt should
call upon him for advice in the purchase of lands as well as
water-power rights for his next cotton mill on the swift River
Derwent. He had also taken William's advice regarding the
apprenticeship of his son Samuel and had engaged the boy for
a trial period. Shortly thereafter, as William was binding a
load of hay, the rope broke. He fell backwards off the wagon
and was fatally injured. When Samuel asked him to arrange
for a formal indenture he replied, "You must do that business
yourself, Samuel; I have so much to do and so little time to do
it in." A few days later, the sturdy English yeoman passed
away at the age of fifty-four.

It was the boy's first major crisis; he faced the facts and in
so doing revealed his inheritance of the tough Slater strain of
realistic approach to the problems of life.

There was much to be considered, and this at a difficult period in his life and for the first time without his father's guidance. With foresight and common sense unusual to a point of rarity in a boy of his age, he began the challenging task of deciding what he must do and the best way to do it.

At the time of the birth of Samuel Slater, the early stages of the invention of machine methods for the carding and spinning of yarn were under way. The crude models were made with timber frames and wooden cogwheels and had very few parts of metal. Yet they gave promise of success in simulating the deft touch of human fingers and the precise timing of muscular effort that our ancestors had performed since prehistoric time, as they spun yarn for their clothing. The clever English mechanics who made these models did not realize that they had started the Industrial Revolution, with its factory system upon which our modern industrial economy is based. The period of inventive activity continued, and as more successful machines were developed, a novel establishment was created— the factory. Factories were huge places for the quantity production of goods by machine. These were soon to replace the numerous home-shops where goods in small, individual quantities, but of immense aggregate volume, had been made by hand for generations—in the villages and on the farms of the thriving handicraft textile centers of England.

Historians define the three major factors that caused the Industrial Revolution as: the invention of textile machinery, the invention of the Watt steam engine, and the discovery that iron ore could be smelted by the use of coke.

Rejecting these definitions, in his "Education in Our Industrial Society" (*Technology Review,* February 1957), William R. Hawthorne, University of Cambridge, says: "Whatever the reasons for the suddenness with which the industrial era started, it was not the result of a series of inventions randomly achieved by unschooled mechanics supported by greedy entrepreneurs. . . . It is new not because men's minds are sharper, but because the intellectual energy previously devoted to philosophical speculation about man's spirit and man's place in the universe has been directed to understanding nature itself and the artifacts which we ourselves have built."

The machines of the early factories were driven by water wheels. Thus the factories were located in the rural areas, where good water-power sites were to be found, such as those along the River Derwent. When it became increasingly difficult to recruit a sufficient supply of mill operatives to work in the rural areas, steam gave the answer, for it could supply power miles from any water-power site. Huge steam-powered factories therefore arose in Manchester and other English cities, where labor was plentiful. With the discovery that they could substitute coke for the charcoal derived from the sadly depleted forests, the foundries and forges became able to increase their production of iron. The textile industry was a ready market, for better machines could be made from cast-iron or wrought-iron, and wooden members could be largely dispensed with. There was the corollary stimulus toward greater accuracy in machine-tool methods, which was of immense advantage to all industry: textile, iron, and the rest.

Samuel Slater was born a few months before Watt secured the patent for his steam engine, and one year before a patent (later annulled) was granted to Richard Arkwright for his famous spinning machine, which was called the water-frame because it was driven by water power. Distinguished names in the archives of textile history are those of the ingenious men who contributed to the ultimate success of the machine methods—Kay (flying shuttle), Wyatt, Paul, High (early spinning models), Hargreaves (spinning jenny), Crompton (mule spinner), Cartwright (power loom, years later), and Arkwright, whose unified system of carding, roving, drawing, and spinning was to achieve the greatest success, thanks to the early financial support of Jedediah Strutt.

In 1769, Arkwright built the world's first spinning mill at Hockley, near Nottingham Market. Here he strove to perfect his water frame, which was coupled temporarily to horses as prime movers. Since he needed money, he entered into a partnership with Jedediah Strutt, then a prosperous manufacturer of ribbed stockings in Derby. The partnership was a success. In 1771, it built the world's first water-powered spinning mill at Cromford on the River Derwent, and in 1776, built another mill a few miles south in Belper, which Strutt took over when the partnership was dissolved.

Samuel's brief probation in the business of machine spinning had made him wish to continue; but an apprenticeship was a serious proposition that had to be carefully considered and he went at the problem with a serious, far-sighted consideration which, from modern standards, seems almost incredible. He reasoned this way: if he divided his present age by two, the

16

ORIGINAL INDENTURES OF APPRENTICESHIP

Samuel Slater to Jedediah Strutt, dated January 8, 1883. Size of original indentures paper, 8½″ x 6″.

➤

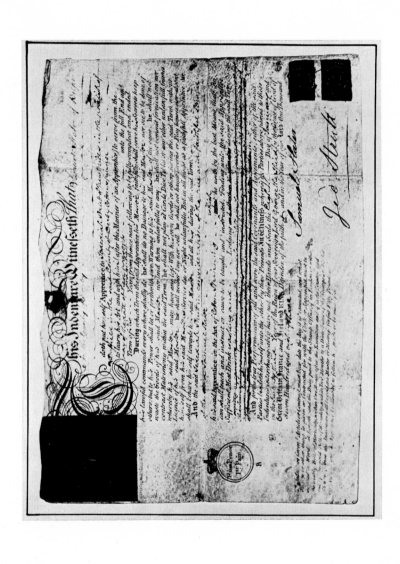

result would be the number of years that he must serve as an apprentice—too many years to waste in a business that might not be successful. He needed to know more about the prospects. So this young boy of fourteen went to the mature businessman Strutt and discussed the future of this new industry, then confined to a relatively small district in the English Midlands. What was its future? Would it be worthwhile for him to spend the next seven years of his life in preparation? Would it be a permanent business? And Strutt, who later made a fortune in it, gave his contemporary opinion.

"It is not probable, Samuel," he said, "that it will always be as good as it is now, but I have no doubt it will always be a fair business, if it be well managed."

This was what Samuel wanted to know and the discussion finished, Samuel made his decision: he would sign an indenture whereby he would become an apprentice with Jedediah Strutt as his master.

"If it be well managed," Strutt had said. There is no question of his managerial ability. He taught Samuel many of the principles of good management which were later exhibited and which paid off in high dividends when Strutt's apprentice had his own business to conduct.

2

"THIS INDENTURE WITNESSETH That Samuel Slater of Belper in the County of Derby doth put himself Apprentice to Jedediah Strutt of New Mills in the Parish of Duffield in the said County of Derby Cotton Spinner to learn his Art and with him (after the Manner of an Apprentice) to serve from the day of the date of these presents unto the full End and Term of Six Years and an half from thence next following to be fully compleat and ended. . . . "

So reads the first paragraph of the indenture of Samuel Slater to Jedediah Strutt. It is dated "the Eighth Day of January and in the Twenty Third Year of the Reign of our Sovereign Lord *George The Third* by the Grace of God of Great Britain, France and Ireland *King* Defender of the faith &c and in the Year of our *Lord* One Thousand Seven Hundred and Eighty Three." The indenture therefore bears the date of the year George the Third acknowledged the independence of thirteen of his American Colonies, officially ending the American War of Independence.

The indenture was signed by Apprentice Samuel Slater, fourteen and one-half years of age, and by his Master, Jedediah Strutt, who was fifty-seven years old. Samuel was growing up, and the same hard common sense that had prompted his precocious cross-examination of Strutt on the prospects of cotton

18

spinning made him read very carefully the terms of this small parchment that called for the almost body-and-soul sale of Samuel to Strutt. Its requirements were given in terms archaic even in the year 1783, for the form of an indenture had not been altered since the Statute of Apprentices of 1532, with its harsh apprenticeship terms.

"During which Term," the indenture stipulates, "the said Apprentice his Master faithfully shall serve his Secreets keep his lawful commands every where gladly do he shall do no Damage to his said Master nor see to be done of others; but to his Power shall let or forthwith give Warning to his said Master of the same. he shall not waste the Goods of his said Master nor lend them unlawfully to any. he shall not commit fornication nor contract Matrimony within the said Term. he shall not play at Cards Dice Tables or any other unlawfull Games whereby his said Master may have any loss With his own Goods or others during the said Term without Licence of his said Master. he shall netiher buy nor sell he shall not haunt Taverns or Play houses nor absent himself from his said Masters Service day or Night unlawfully But in all things as a faithfull Apprentice he shall behave himself towards his said Master and all his during the said Term.

And the said Jedediah Strutt in consideration of the true and faithful Service of the said Samuel Slater his said Apprentice in the Art of Cotton Spinning which he useth by the best Means, that he can shall teach and instruct or cause to be taught and instructed. Finding unto the said Apprentice Sufficient Meat Drink washing and Lodging during the said Term and in And for the true Performances of all and every the said Covenants and Agreements, either of the said Parties bindeth himself unto the other by these Presents In Witness whereof the Parties above named to these Indentures interchangeably have put their Hands and Seals. . . . . "

No mention is made of clothing for Samuel during his six and one-half years of service, nor of any payment in money at the end, to give the apprentice a start in life, for such kindness was unthought of in the year 1783. There is evidence that Samuel had judged well in accepting Strutt as master, however, for the latter seems to have become almost a second father to the son of his deceased friend. More than loyalty to his departed friend caused Strutt's kindness, of course, for he knew that he could use this intelligent boy to their mutual advantage. Shrewd Jedediah Strutt was a good judge of men —and boys.

He and his sons were credited with changing Belper from an inconsiderable place into a prosperous, industrial community during a few decades, as their cotton mills were developed. Old Belper had been a farming area, its only industrial products consisting of handmade horse nails of a superior quality, and pottery. Under the Strutts, it had increased twenty-fold and had the facilities that went with its size—it became a market town; the London-Manchester post coaches passed through it; a horse-mail carried letters from it to Derby, daily; and its many houses were substantially built of stone. As might be expected its pottery and nail trade had increased, although it was feared that soon machinery would seal the fate of the nail trade in Belper. Predominating all industrial activities was cotton.

The early age at which Slater started to work in Strutt's factory provides a striking example of the contemporary status

20

of child labor. For his day, he was not an abused juvenile; in fact, his age of fourteen and one-half years would classify him as one of the older boys in the mill.

The engagement of small children in the new factories of England was only an extension of the generations-old custom of putting them to work early at farm tasks and in the home-located shops which dotted the English countryside. This custom is easy to understand. In a period when there was little mechanical power, with most of the work to be done manually, as many hands must be used as possible; and there were many processes for which the tiny hands of children were adequate.

Many years were to elapse before the harsh working conditions and long hours of child labor were alleviated. Nineteen years after the date of Slater's indenture, an early step toward the correction of these evils was taken. At that time, Parliament passed an act that forbade the employment of persons in factories or mines who were less than nine years of age. In 1833, it was enacted that children under thirteen should not work more than forty-eight hours a week, and those under eighteen not more than sixty-eight hours a week.

The Strutt mills and the fine stone cottages built for the mill workers in rural Belper and Milford were to become noted for their excellence, compared with the less humanely designed mills and the squalid living quarters erected in some English locations during the early days of the Industrial Revolution.

Samuel resided with Strutt, in the latter's home in Milford. For a sturdy boy, Strutt's home was an easy walking distance from Holly House: about two miles to the bridge which crossed the River Derwent at Belper, then along the tree-lined country road by the river to Longwalls Lane, and up the steep approach to the Slater home. Yet it is recorded that Samuel went six months without seeing his family, preferring to spend his Sundays studying the spinning equipment in the Strutt mill.

Like any boy in rural England he was fascinated by the cleverly built series of machines that would spin yarn of good quality. Since his childhood he had watched his mother and sisters spin yarn at home which was of no better quality. There were differences, of course, perhaps the most noticeable being the noise of the machines—from the whirring pulleys of wood, the grinding clash of ill-fitting iron gears, and the slapping impact of the rope drives. There was an aggressive quality to the mill noises, far different from the gentle cadence of the Holly House spinning wheels. The noises were symbolic of the inexorably harsh tenor of the change from the handicraft methods to those of the machines. The boy, of course, did not realize this. Years later, as an adult, he would take steps to alleviate the disturbing impact of the confined factory routine on the spirit of the open-air country youths who were to work for him in America.

Magically, after the raw cotton had been hand-cleaned into bunting, a series of machines turned it into yarn. The apprentice must learn the function of each machine and be able to tend them all—these wooden robots bearing the titles of breaker card, lap machine, finisher card, drawing frame, lantern, or can-roving frame, bobbin winding wheel (hand operated), spinning frame, with its long rows of spindles, and reel, which wound the finished yarn into skeins or hanks, ready for the hand loom of the weaver.*

---

* *See* Notes 2 and 3, Appendix A, pp. 181-84.

The machines were very crude compared with the standards of today. They were mounted on timber frames and had wooden cogwheels, and for some functions cords were used for belts. Iron members were used only where essential, not only because iron was expensive, but because of the lack of adequate machine-tool methods to process it. At the time of the introduction of apprentice Samuel Slater to the textile machines, the world's first spinning mill was only fourteen years old; about as old as the boy himself. There were many breakdowns and a continuing program of improvements, in which the young apprentice played a part. One very desirable improvement was a device to distribute the spun yarn on the spindle more properly. Observing Strutt's difficulty in creating such a device, Samuel designed a wooden heart-motion cam that, when operated by a cord belt from the driving shaft, raised and lowered the row of spindles slowly at speeds that would accomplish this end. In appreciation of this evidence of the mechanical ingenuity of his apprentice, Jedediah gave the boy one guinea, then a substantial sum.

All of the ingenious devices of spinners and carders would be useless but for the power of the sturdy River Derwent that drove them. Dependable water power was essential to the successful operation of textile mills, Samuel learned. Until near the end of his life when the steam engine began to supersede the water wheel, he made sure of an adequate flow and head of the streams where his various ventures were to be located.

Samuel Slater, now a valuable apprentice, grew up with the early textile phase of the Industrial Revolution in England, as the defects of its crude apparatus were gradually corrected.

As his apprenticeship neared its end, Samuel, nearly twenty-one years old, began to think about his next step into the future.

While the textile industry of England was making rapid strides because of the successful machine methods, handicraft methods still prevailed in America in this period, a few years after the Revolutionary War. Farseeing American statesmen and men of business realized the industrial limitations and took aggressive steps to correct them. Their efforts were concentrated on securing plans or models of the English machine carders and spinners, despite the rigid laws of that country to restrict the disclosure of the successful processes. The newspaper account of a liberal bounty (£100) granted by the Legislature of Pennsylvania to a man who had only partially succeeded in constructing a model of a carding machine and rollers of a spinning machine had somehow reached England, even in that day of limited communication. We can imagine the head-shaking of English businessmen who read about this in their coffee-house newspaper, where it was actually illegal for it to have been printed. Having conceded defeat in the revolution of their former American colonies, they were determined that these unruly people should not obtain knowledge of the methods that were beginning to make many Englishmen prosperous. But they talked, and the news reached Derbyshire, and even the spinners in little Belper learned that their newly acquired knowledge of the machine methods could be of great value in America. Eagerly, the spinners and apprentices of Belper talked over their chances of a better job in America.

Samuel Slater listened and kept his own counsel. His

spinner friends wondered about the possibilities of a mechanic-emigrant to America ever getting out of England. All countries, France, Sweden, Russia, Holland, Prussia, and, of course, the United States, were trying to learn the English textile processes, particularly the ways of building the equipment for them. Since 1695-96 when the export of stocking frames had been prohibited, the list of the Acts of Parliament which forbade the export of machinery and the enticing of workmen had been lengthened, in the attempt to keep English mechanics and the machines they operated at home. To the cotton spinners, these were bad laws; they shrugged their shoulders, in the Anglo-Saxon spirit that felt that unjust laws were written to be disobeyed. And Samuel just listened.

There is no question but what the idea of going to America held a challenging appeal to a young man going on twenty-one, but it is characteristic of Slater's integrity that he never harbored the idea of leaving until his apprenticeship should be over. He remained faithful to his master's interests, then his indenture over, he went about the preparations for his future with his usual thoughtful foresightedness.

No matter where he decided to start his operations he needed more experience in guiding the work of others, and should he decide to go to America there was much to be done first. Since no plans or models could be taken with him, there was nothing to do except memorize every detail of the intricate spinning machines which that country wanted so much.

Once more he turned to his friend Strutt and asked him for a job which would give him the added advantage of executive experience. Strutt gladly "gave him oversight" over the erection of some new equipment. This was probably at Strutt's new mill at Milford, a few miles south of Belper, on the River Derwent.

Slowly, Samuel reasoned with himself as to his next step. Fully aware of the risk he would be taking if he decided to leave England, he knew that nothing was more important than that he maintain the most rigid secrecy. This was probably less difficult for Slater that it would be for some, since he was secretive by nature. Still, it must have been hard not to be able to talk it over with Strutt as he so often had done when faced with a decision. There was his family, too, his mother and his brothers and sisters, all of whom would probably have tried to dissuade him from taking such a big risk. Literally his decision was made in the secret meditation of heart of a determined young man whose certainty, once his mind was made up, would brook no interruption by well-meaning friends. He would go to America, land of promise to so many Englishmen of his generation. To this end he began to make preparation.

When his time came to go, September 1, 1789, Samuel went first to Holly House. Whatever misgivings he might have had, his determination sustained him as he viewed, with more scrutiny than on the casual visits during his indenture, the main house and its pleasant surroundings. Even when he met his mother, Elizabeth, who after six years of widowhood had married again, he did not weaken in his resolve to guard his secret. He merely explained: "I am going by stage to London, and have come to put together my clothes for the trip." He never saw her again.

From this date he must no longer be called the youthful Samuel. He has to be called Samuel Slater, a potential businessman, prematurely grown to the stature of an adult, youthful only in the measure of his years.

London was one hundred and thirty-four miles southeast of Belper. It seems probable that Samuel Slater caught the Manchester stage on its return trip to the metropolis, an up-to-date coach with springs, and with seats on the roof—all told, good for fourteen persons. It was also a fast coach, averaging —allowing for stops at night—forty miles per day; so Slater had to spend two or three nights at taverns along the way.

In the low-ceilinged taverns, the passengers talked of the possible danger of highwaymen, to whom prosperous stage-coach riders were profitable prey. Only eight years earlier, three highwaymen had been hung in Norwich, one hundred miles to the east.

While waiting in London for the captain of his sailing vessel to make up his mind on when to depart, Slater decided to see the sights of the city—its cathedrals, Westminster Abbey, and St. Paul's, the old Tower of London, and other attractions. From a distance, he saw finely dressed lords and ladies. He also glimpsed the sordid side of London life—drunkenness in the poorer sections, where certain of the gin shops, not so many years earlier, had invited passers-by to get drunk for a penny, or dead drunk for twopence.

Slater had one sobering experience in London which probably made a lasting impression on him and made him realize that in the world outside the small town of Belper were people who had no scruples about taking advantage of a greenhorn. In fact, when Slater told of the incident himself, he said it served to "sharpen his eye-teeth." On one of his rambles through the city, dressed, of course, in his country clothes, he was accosted by a man who drew him to one side and told him in a confidential manner that he had some silk stockings that he would sell remarkably low, but that he wished the bargain to be "just between ourselves." Young Slater was confident that he had found a real buy and bought the stockings. Delighted with his first purchase in the big city, he hurried to his lodgings to examine his prize. We may imagine his chagrin when he found that he had bought stockings without any feet!

When, in a week or so, the captain had set the date of embarkation, Samuel Slater rushed to a London coaching-inn and posted the letter to his mother which he had written days earlier. "I am going to America," was the substance of it. It was dated September 13, 1789.

Poor mother Elizabeth! Her first reaction upon receipt of the letter was probably one of anger at the half-truth of his deception, anger at this strange, big son whom she had begotten. Then, knowing of the brutal hardships of the long voyage on the rough Atlantic, she worried about him—so many sailing ships never made their destination—and she prayed hard for the safe passage of her son.

By later, intimate family correspondence that has been preserved, it can be seen that Elizabeth came to understand her son better. She decided, when she learned of his romantic courtship of young Hannah Wilkinson and his marriage to her, that her intensely businesslike son was a very human young man. She sensed his natural humanity when in the agony of a bereft young parent, he wrote her of the death of her grandchildren, a boy, named for her husband, and two little girls—one of them her namesake.

3

THE PROCEDURE OF the emigration of Englishmen to America after the Revolutionary War was usually as follows: when the port official of London or some other port scanned the list of passengers given to him by the master of the outgoing vessel, he would find them listed as merchants, farmers, or laborers, all of which classes were exempt from the law's restrictions on emigration. Since no mechanics or manufacturers were allowed to leave, they found none listed as such.

If the official found that a man was misrepresenting his occupation, it merely meant that the ship could not sail until the man had been put ashore. Although legally he stood a chance of being kept in custody until the next assizes, apparently this step was seldom taken. The teeth of the law— fines or imprisonment—were kept for the more serious offenders: those who were attempting to take manufacturing models or plans out of the country or those who were trying to smuggle out the mechanics to build and operate the machines.

When the word was passed around that the port officers were unusually alert, there were rowboats or little sailing vessels ready, for a proper stipend, to carry emigrant mechanics to the ship after it had cleared port. There is the story of the mechanic who had taken advantage of this practical arrangement after putting his wife on board, but who unfortunately had had to leave his chest of tools behind.

There is therefore a sound basis of fact in the legend that Samuel Slater sailed from London as a farm laborer, taking the advice of friends who knew how the ill-conceived law could be circumvented, particularly by a young man of his ruddy complexion that savored of the outdoor life of a farmer.

As a fellow passenger, his shipmates found him likable, but not talkative—a man who could keep his own business to himself, while still making friends. Only a fool, or a man with something to hide, would keep wholly to himself throughout the acute discomforts of a voyage from England to the United States in this year 1789. In September, as the ship left London, he admired with other "farm laborers," indentured servants, or merchants with American commitments, the antics of the gliding gulls, soaring without effort above the gray-green surges of the West Coast seas. He discussed with his friends the probable length of the voyage—perhaps two months. They agreed that they were really not going to a foreign country— it was merely another English community, calling itself the United States of America.

A tall young man, he had to learn to keep his head low, as he entered the low-ceilinged bunk room. He controlled his disgust at the poor food. He wrapped his cloak about him against the cold blasts of the North Atlantic winds. As well as he could, he maintained a personal privacy of habits, under conditions where there was little privacy. Therefore, he was particularly cautious, as he opened his trunk for an occasional change of garment, not to reveal the only document that he took with him to America: his indenture to Jedediah Strutt. His friends, getting to know him better during the rough voyage, noted his interest in such mechanical matters as the crude rigging apparatus, and how the captain tried to check his dead reckoning of the position of the ship with the navigational apparatus of the day. His shipmates undoubtedly noticed however, that he sometimes carried himself aloof from the normal shipboard chatter. So often, he would gaze musingly across the vast expanse of the Atlantic. It was his own business, of course, and his friends had an equal desire to be left alone occasionally as they planned their first move, once landed in New York after this bitterly hard voyage to America. All, of course, agreed that the hardships were worthwhile; they were going to America, the Mecca of many ambitious English young men.

Samuel was a big man, with an intellectual countenance that revealed no signs of the aggressiveness concealed behind the pleasant face. As to his apparent dreaming, it is obvious that he was merely going over in his mind the dimensions and arrangements of these novel English machines for the carding and spinning of cotton, and the way they were operated. With it all, Samuel Slater was undoubtedly a reserved yet friendly young man who won both the respect and friendship of his fellow passengers.

With so much time for contemplation, he wondered about these Americans with whom he would soon have to work. He thought of them, of course, as Englishmen living under different conditions, having to solve the problems of frontier life, and for those in the hinterlands, having to fight the Indians whose territory they were usurping. He soon learned that their independent spirit came from a manner of living that had no place for the caste system of England, and that one man was as good as another, be he of the rank that corresponded to that of duke, lord, or yeoman farmer, like his father, in England. Such time-filling meditations always ended with one comfortable reflection: that of the strong possibility of success in America for a man of his experience.

He had but one plan. He would seek people who spun cotton and might employ a man who knew how to build and operate the Arkwright spinning equipment.

II
Young Manhood
1789-1801

1

RISING ABOVE THE FLAT sea coast of New Jersey, the steep
bluff of Navesink was sighted by the captain, and he told the
sea-weary passengers that they would soon enter the spacious
harbor of New York. By an interesting coincidence, the dates
of departure and arrival of the ship closely matched those of
the *Mayflower*. Both voyages took sixty-six days. Slater left
London on September 13; the *Mayflower* left Plymouth, England, on September 6, one hundred and sixty-nine years earlier.
Slater landed in New York on November 18; the *Mayflower*
docked at the site of Provincetown, Massachusetts, on November 11. September is considered about the worst month for a
westerly passage under sail. Since the *Mayflower* trip, it is
probable that there had been little change, by Slater's time, in
the horrible conditions under which emigrants sailed.

He had planned to seek work in Philadelphia, largest city
in America and the metropolis of the State of Pennsylvania,
where the bounty promised for the construction of Arkwright
carders had first tempted him to emigrate to America. Within
four days of his arrival, however, he had obtained lodging at
No. 37 Golden Hill, and had accepted a job with the New
York Manufacturing Company on Vesey Street, in lower
Manhattan.

The New York Manufacturing Company was just another of the several textile ventures the promoters of which sought, in the decade after the Revolutionary War, to imitate the English methods for the machine spinning of yarn, inspired by the huge profits that would come to those who succeeded. It was a newly organized company, and its promoters were undoubtedly very happy to find an Englishman whose indenture certificate proved that he should be proficient in these processes.

They smiled at the Derbyshire accent of this young man, as they led him to the machines they had assembled for their new business. They had little to show him: one card, two "machines," and two spinning jennies that young Slater considered worthless.

As to the water power that they depended upon to drive the machines, if they really were driven by a water wheel, Slater was in a position to tell them that the puny flow and fall of a spring-fed brook in this level area near the tip of Manhattan Island could not supply adequate power for any but the tiniest of spinning frames. (It is more probable that the apparatus of the New York Manufacturing Company was powered by husky men, and that the account that mentions Slater's dissatisfaction with their water power is in error.)

It was Slater's first American disappointment, but why cry over spilt milk, he concluded. Already he had begun to make friends, one of whom was a Captain Brown whose packet sailed between New York and Providence, Rhode Island. It was to him that Slater turned in his disappointment. The captain told him of a prominent, deeply religious Yankee-Quaker, Moses Brown, of Providence, whose family had played a leading role in Rhode Island history since colonial times, and who was connected with the firm of Almy & Brown, a machine-spinning concern there. Slater decided to try him next.

On December 2, 1789, a few weeks after his arrival in New York, Samuel Slater sat down to write a letter—a major operation then, more than one and a half centuries ago. It was addressed to "Mr. Brown, Providence." Of course the goose-quill pen needed sharpening; pens always did. Mr. Jackson, his teacher back in Belper, had admonished him never to start writing until the pen was in order, and so, as a good penman, Slater first "mended his pen." He trimmed the pen's stiff point with his knife, and tried it on a scrap of the same precious handmade paper as that on which he was to write. The pewter sander was handy, ready for blotting what he was to write.

Of the recorded letters of Samuel Slater this one to Moses Brown appears to be that of the earliest date. Paraphrased in today's terminology, it becomes an excellent, respectful modern sales letter. Moses Brown, with a substantial investment in defective cotton machinery on his hands, must have considered the letter in the Biblical terms of "manna from heaven," provided the young man who wrote it could back up his claims:

New York, December 2d, 1789
Sir, — A few days ago I was informed that you wanted a manager of *cotton spinning*, & c. in which business I flatter myself that I can give the greatest satisfaction, in making machinery, making good yarn, either for *stockings* or *twist*, as any that is made in England; as I have had opportunity, and oversight, of Sir Richard Arkwright's works, and in Mr. Strutt's mill upwards of eight years. If you are not provided for, should be

37

glad to serve you; though I am in the New York manufactory, and have been for three weeks since I arrived from England. But we had but *one card, two machines* two spinning jennies, which I think are not worth using. My encouragement is pretty good, but should much rather have the care of the perpetual carding and spinning. *My intention* is to erect a *perpetual card and spinning.* (Meaning the Arkwright patents.) If you please to drop a line respecting the amount of encouragement you wish to give, by favour of Captain Brown, you will much oblige, sir, your most obedient humble servant,

SAMUEL SLATER

N.B.—Please to direct to me at No. 37, Golden Hill, New York,
Mr. Brown, Providence

Brown's reply "by favour of the captain" promised a pretty tempting compensation:

Providence, 10th 12th month, 1789

Friend, — I received thine of 2d inst. and observe its contents. I, or rather Almy & Brown, who has the business in the cotton line, which I began, one being my son-in-law, and the other a kinsman, want the assistance of a person skilled in the frame or water spinning. An experiment has been made, which has failed, no person being acquainted with the business, and the frames imperfect.

We are destitute of a person acquainted with waterframe spinning; thy being already engaged in a factory with many able proprietors, we can hardly suppose we can give the encouragement adequate to leaving thy present employ. As the frame we have is the first attempt of the kind that has been made in America, it is too imperfect to afford much encouragement; we

38

hardly know what to say to thee, but if thou couldst perfect and conduct them to profit, if thou wilt come and do it, thou shalt have all the profits made of them over and above the interest of the money they cost, and the wear and tear of them. We will find stock and be repaid in yarn as we may agree, for six months. And this we do for the information thou can give, if fully acquainted with the business. After this, if we find the business profitable, we can enlarge it, or before, if sufficient proof of it be had on trial, and can make any further agreement that may appear best or agreeable on all sides. We have secured only a temporary water convenience, but if we find the business profitable, can perpetuate one that is convenient. If thy prospects should be better, and thou should know of any other person unengaged, should be obliged to thee to mention us to him. In the mean time, shall be glad to be informed whether thou come or not. If thy present situation does not come up to what thou wishest, and, from thy knowledge of the business, can be ascertained of the advantages of the mills so as to induce thee to come and work ours, and have the *credit* as well as advantage of perfecting the first water-mill in America, we should be glad to engage thy care so long as they can be made profitable to both, and we can agree. I am, for myself and Almy & Brown, thy friend,

Moses Brown

Samuel Slater, at 37, Golden Hill, New York.

2

No RAILROAD LINE ran from New York to Providence (not, in fact, until several years after Slater's death). Stagecoach travel in America was uncertain of schedule, and about as uncomfortable a means of transport as the sailing vessel that had brought him from England, so Slater undoubtedly traveled by water from New York to Providence. Probably he sailed in the packet of his friend Captain Brown whose experience enabled him to steer clear of dangerous Hell Gate Reef, and to navigate safely up Long Island Sound into the western passage of Narragansett Bay and north to Providence.

There was plenty of time during the trip for Slater to study the long letter he had received from Moses Brown. It was a straightforward epistle that made one respect its writer; surely Moses Brown should prove to be a safe man to work with.

As they shook hands in Providence, the two men made the first, quick appraisal common to persons meeting for the first time. Slater noted the flat-crowned hat, its wide brim shading a kindly face; the Roman nose and sharp chin; the aura of whitening hair reaching to the shoulders of the older man's voluminous coat. He noticed, possibly with some amusement at first, the "thee's" and "thou's" of the older man's speech.

He later learned that Moses Brown, who was thirty years his senior, had little vigor of speech or movement, and had quit

40

his more active business responsibilities because of failing health; a partial invalidism that was to continue for nearly half a century. Slater learned also that Brown was wealthy, and was highly regarded in Providence because of his public and business interests.

Brown was impressed with the frank features of this respectful young man and with his manner of promptly getting down to business. He read each word of the precious indenture and did not conceal his respect for its record of the long experience of Slater in the operations of spinning under the mastership of Strutt, who had been a partner of the great Arkwright. But is this young man enough of a mechanic to adapt my imperfect spinning frames to the designs of Arkwright? he wondered. Obviously, his kinsman, Sylvanus Brown, should be able to decide upon the ability of this confident young Englishman, for Sylvanus, who lived in nearby Pawtucket where the equipment of Almy & Brown was located, was a skilled mechanic. "Thou must come with me to Pawtucket where they are set up," Moses said, concluding the interview.

When Slater reached Pawtucket, he found it to be a tiny place. Yet this settlement of a few buildings had its reputation. It was considered the workshop of the surrounding villages because of the proficiency of the ingenious mechanics who lived there. They were able successors of the Englishman Joseph Jenks, who was a noted worker in brass and iron, and in early colonial time had built an iron forge in a deep ravine below Pawtucket Falls. Here he had made iron utensils and tools which found a ready market in nearby Providence. For his water power, Jenks undoubtedly had merely tapped with

41

a dug-canal the waters above one of the several jagged ledges in the river, called at various times the Pawtucket River (after the Indian designation for "falls of water"), the Seekonk River, or the Blackstone River.

Other dams that partially spanned the river had followed, as the demand for water power had grown, and in the year 1718 some of the upper ledges forming the falls had been united to make a full-width dam extending from the east to the west bank of the river. A few years earlier, a canal on the west bank named Sargeant's Trench had been built to enable the shad and alewives to reach their spawning areas upstream, during freshets. As a fishway, this channel proved unsuccessful, and it became a millrace to deliver water power from above the new dam to a few little mills along the west bank. This was the source of power for the cotton mill for which Moses Brown had secured temporary water-power rights, as mentioned in his letter to Slater.

When they arrived at the home of Sylvanus Brown, on January 17, 1790, Moses introduced Slater to his kinsman: "Sylvanus, I have brought to thee a young man who says he knows how to spin cotton; I want thee to keep him tonight and talk to him, and see what he can do." In the morning, Sylvanus told Moses that Slater seemed to know the practical side of the business, and they went to view the machines for the production of cotton yarn that Almy & Brown had assembled.

Knowing that others had called them worth nothing more than so much old iron, Moses was not surprised when Slater said, "These will not do; they are good for nothing in their present condition nor can they be made to answer." As Slater pointed out the defects that made it impossible for the machines to spin properly, and drew convincing oral pictures of the Arkwright devices that had such a famous record of success, he not only convinced the older man of his knowledge of machine-spinning apparatus, but he imbued Brown with his own confidence. So sure Slater was of his ability to build the machinery with no drawings, patterns, or models from which to work that Brown became positive also, to the point where he hired him. He proposed that Slater should duplicate the Arkwright models at a wage of $1.00 per day. Slater's ensuing success is a matter of record and becomes more impressive when compared with the record of the failures of many attempts to copy the English machines during the decade of intensive efforts that had preceded his arrival in America.

With one or two exceptions, and these imperfect, the machines before Slater lacked the Arkwright devices which had been used in England for several years. They reveal an impressive record, however, of the driving urge of Americans to catch up with England's machine methods, since Christopher Tully is supposed to have successfully constructed a Hargreaves type of jenny at Philadelphia, in the year 1775, that would spin yarn after a fashion.

The partial success of Tully had led to the establishment of a textile business by Samuel Wetherill, Jr., at Philadelphia, which had furnished clothing to the Continental Army, mostly hand-spun and with the weaving performed in private homes. A supposedly incendiary fire ended the venture of Wetherill, in which no Arkwright-type machines were involved, a few months after Slater appeared in Pawtucket.

In Massachusetts, the active attempts at machine spinning seem to have been intensified during the three years preceding the arrival of Slater. Scottish brothers, Robert and Alexander Barr, had been employed by Hugh Orr at Bridgewater, Massachusetts, to construct a spinning jenny, a stock card, and a roping machine. The Massachusetts legislature awarded £200 for this effort. Thomas Somers, versed in spinning methods in England, and granted £20, produced an imperfect Arkwright spinning frame. Various New Englanders viewed the Barr and Somers attempts when exhibited by Orr, and the equipment became known as the State's Models.

They were on exhibit to all who were interested. Unlike the British, the Yankees were not secretive; visitors were allowed to make as many drawings of the State's Models as they wished. Meanwhile, during this short period of intense effort to produce workable Arkwright-type machines, a cotton factory was started by John Cabot and Joshua Fisher on Bass River, at Beverly, Massachusetts. Some suppose that their equipment was copied from the State's Models; others say that it was imported. Started a few months prior to Slater's sailing from London, this Beverly plant claims the distinction of being the first textile mill to be erected in America, although another record indicates that the Wetherill Mill in Philadelphia preceded that in Beverly by twelve days! The Beverly mill was not successful, however, due to imperfections in its machines and its manufacture of rather poor products. It would soon cease operations, unable to produce at a profit, despite its receipt of State aid from time to time.

About a year before Slater's sailing, Rhode Island entered the picture when Daniel Anthony, Andrew Dexter, and Lewis

Peck, having obtained drawings of the State's Models at Bridgewater, constructed a jenny of twenty-eight spindles, a carding machine, and a spinning frame of thirty-two spindles —apparently at Providence. Also in this year, two Scotsmen, James McKerris and Joseph Alexander, proficient in the knowledge of the fly shuttle, set up shop with their loom in the markethouse there, but they soon gave up. A State's Model spinning frame was set up at East Greenwich and also proved unsuccessful. An Irish stocking weaver, John Fuller, had set up a loom at East Greenwich that he would soon be glad to sell.

Moses Brown seems to have kept track of the always unsuccessful attempts to introduce machine-spinning apparatus in America. Patriotically, he wanted American industry to catch up with the demand for manufactured goods, and as a shrewd business man, he saw a way to make money. Finally, he bought carding and spinning equipment which appeared to have some promise of success. His intent was good, but before we call his judgment poor in his selection, we have to admit that he had little to choose from in this period of scant information from which to work, because of the English secrecy and the limited facilities of the Yankee artisans who tried to build the machines.

A few months prior to the coming of Slater, Moses Brown had turned this equipment over to the firm of Almy & Brown to operate. The partners of the firm were William Almy, a son-in-law of Moses, and a "kinsman," Smith Brown. Moses Brown merely supplied the capital. The poor quality of the machines is shown by the fact that most of the spinning of the mixed cotton and linen goods produced had been carried on by hand in the adjacent cellars or on the first floors of the local dwellings.

Although the record is not wholly clear, it appears that ten weeks were spent by Slater in attempts to utilize successfully the two Almy & Brown spinning frames that approximated the Arkwright models. During this period it was decided that the preparatory machines were not worth the effort to make them work. Slater had begun to exhibit his remarkable memory in recalling the many dimensions of the English machines and showed a mechanical ability that would enable him to reproduce them. It will be seen that he also exhibited a business foresight that was unusual in a man of twenty-one in accepting terms that have been criticized as unfair in the distribution of the profits between him and Almy & Brown.

On April 5, 1790, an agreement was made for Slater to produce equipment that he knew would produce good yarn.* The agreement called for ". . . spinning of cotton by water, (of which the said Samuel professes himself a workman, well skilled in all its branches;) . . . ."

It was an ideal arrangement in one important respect. The party of the second part, Slater, knew how to construct and operate the machines. Those of the first part, Almy & Brown, had had several years of business experience that should ensure proper methods in the purchase of raw materials and the marketing of the finished product. They had acted as agents for Moses Brown, in the selling of imported goods, trading

---

* *See* Note 4, Appendix A, pp. 184-86.

with the West Indies, buying molasses, and other ventures of the shrewd Yankee.

Certainly, Slater had improved his position by his advance from a wage earner to that of a partner. He undoubtedly must have winced, however, as he read terms that seemed to make him share the price that Almy & Brown had paid for the defective machines, and the term that mentioned the ". . . usual commissions [to Almy & Brown] of two and a half per cent for purchasing of the stock, and four per cent for disposing of the yarn. . . ." Almy & Brown could also charge to expenses the cost of training apprentices whom they might select. His wage of $1.00 per day was also to stop, for there was the clause: ". . . the said Samuel to be at the expense of his own time and board from thence-forward." (There is later indication however, that Slater's wages were continued.)

The agreement was witnessed by men who were soon to be relatives by marriage to Slater: Oziel Wilkinson, as father-in-law, and his son, Abraham Wilkinson.

Slater signed the agreement, saying with a supreme gesture of confident youth: ". . . Under my proposals, if I do not make as good yarn as they do in England, I will have nothing for my services, but will throw the whole of what I have attempted over the bridge." He demanded that the carpenter who was to help him be put under bonds not to steal the patterns or disclose the nature of the work.

As we progress with our study of the career of Samuel Slater, we shall see certain instances when he made decisions that turned out to be landmarks in his progress toward success. His acceptance of this agreement with Almy & Brown is such a landmark. After all, the objectionable clauses were mostly matters of first costs only. They would soon be paid—assuming successful operation. The continuing returns could be great, and his superb confidence would not let him think of failure at this stage.

Two years later the accounts of Almy & Brown and Slater were balanced, and the returns, while moderate (Slater's net share was £419 4s 3.75d, or about $1,400), were sufficient to warrant an expansion of their facilities. Samuel Slater had made a good start.

SLATER CARDING MACHINE, 1790

Original finisher carding machine built by Samuel Slater in Pawtucket, Rhode Island, in 1790, shown as it appears in the Textile Hall after renovation, January 1959. The cotton batting from the breaker card is fed from the roller on the right into the carding machine. After a second carding operation, it emerges from the finisher card in the form of a sliver, a loose roll of fibers, ready for drawing and spinning.

➤

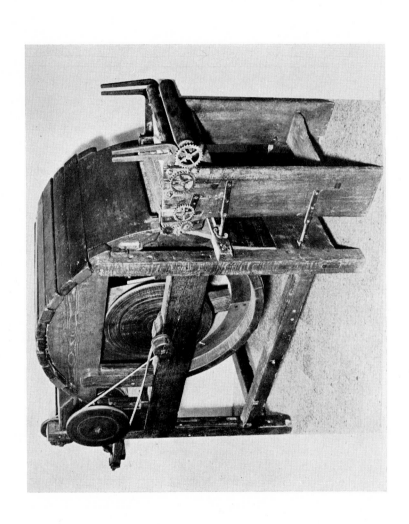

3

AN INSPIRING STORY in the annals of textile history is the account of the success of Samuel Slater in making the first practical reproduction of the Arkwright equipment in America. For their day, the carders and spinners he created were of tremendous complexity, and his feat of memory in recalling the dimensions and functional arrangement of their many elements was phenomenal.

The materials required to build the equipment were limited in the New England of the year 1790, and the mechanics had only crude tools compared to those of today with which to make the various parts. Slater was obliged to exercise his talent in the design of the mechanisms and to sketch them for his able American mechanics to reproduce. He revealed the fact that he also was a good mechanic, since he made tools with which they were to work.

Quaker Lane was a thoroughfare that played an important part in Slater's Pawtucket career. It was here that he boarded with Oziel Wilkinson and his family.

Located two hundred feet from the main street on the east side of the lane, the small shop of Sylvanus Brown became the object of much speculation. Sylvanus had always been respected as a noted wood-worker, and with natural Yankee curiosity, Pawtucket folk wondered what he was up to now; there were shutters on the front windows of the shop and closed blinds covered those in the rear. They saw an energetic young man bearing large and small bundles and heavy sticks of timber. They noted an occasional dray loaded with odd cargo, and an old Negro, Jenks, who frequented the spot. Another regular visitor was Oziel Wilkinson's son David, whose ability in the shaping of iron was notable. Here, behind the closed shutters of the little shop on Quaker Lane, Slater built the basic elements of the Arkwright equipment—the carders and the famous water-frame spinners, with their many ingeniously designed pairs of rollers that made this type so effective. These, with the various preparatory units, were as good copies of the equipment of the Arkwright system as Slater could produce.

Within a few years, as more and more cotton mills were started in New England, following the lead of Slater, it became the practice first to construct the machine shop in which would be made the carders, spinning frames, and looms, which would then be set up on the floors above. Many years elapsed before cotton-producing machinery could be purchased with parts ready-made for assembly.

On the floor of his "machine shop" Samuel Slater traced with chalk the framework of the equipment which Sylvanus Brown cut out from good oak sticks and planed to a smooth finish, before securing the many mortised joints with wooden dowels. Particular care was taken to bore the oak spindles in straight alignment for the iron shafts on which the spindles must turn. As in the English equipment, wooden members were used wherever adequate for the carders and spinning

50

frames that Slater had agreed to make. Iron was too precious for parts where wood would suffice.

In his own shop, David Wilkinson forged what iron parts were used, and turned the shafts of the spindles and the rollers. The many pairs of rollers for the spinning frame intrigued Wilkinson. It was enough for him that Slater had said that they would work, for he respected the young man.

Wilkinson's turning lathe was made mostly of wood, of course. Although contemporary lathes were driven by foot treadles or by hand cranks, it is probable that a cleverly designed connection to the water wheel of Wilkinson's shop, near Carpenter's shop, powered the lathe. Within a decade, the English mechanic Maudsley was to produce his famous slide-rest; and some believe that it is more than probable that ingenious David Wilkinson may have anticipated certain of the Englishman's lathe devices.

Just as a modern coin is milled on its edge, the lower roller of each pair had to be milled to grip the yarn firmly against the leather-mounted surface of the upper roller. The milling was undoubtedly done by hand filing. (Several years would elapse before Eli Whitney invented a milling machine which, next to his cotton gin, was his most famous invention.)

David had watched his mother spin yarn, and he knew that yarn demanded skillful manipulation as it was attenuated, or thinned out, on its way from distaff to spindle. A good mechanic, he could see that this most important drawing-out device of the Arkwright water frame, the roll spinners, should work when held together by the suspended cast-iron weights he had made. He certainly would not have taken on this job if he had not believed in its practicality.

Completing the team that built America's first practical cotton machinery was the elderly Samuel Brunius Jenks, the Negro general helper. He bore the name of the Jenks family that had developed the iron industry of Pawtucket, workshop, with its fine water power, of adjacent Rhode Island towns. It is not too far-fetched to presume that Samuel Brunius had been one of the slaves of Moses Brown whom he had freed when he had joined the Society of Friends seventeen years before.

New England had a few men who were expert in making hand cards, flat pieces of wood as large as an oversized curry comb, mounted with leather and spotted with sharp iron teeth with which to align the fibres of the raw cotton, wool, or flax, before spinning. Another Quaker, Pliny Earle, of Leicester, Massachusetts, who apparently was such a hand-card maker, was engaged for the much more ambitious task of making the cards of the revolving cylinder and also the stationary upper cards of Slater's carding machine. He was inexperienced at this, and he got into trouble.

There were those who furnished the oak and pine stuff; hundreds of hand-threaded screws of various sizes; brads, nails, and rope; and the piece of lignum vitae which weighed thirty-eight pounds—all recorded in the still extant Almy & Brown Day Book from 1789 on.

Samuel Slater had to keep ahead of these assistants; he made sketches, devised tools to build the unusual members, and inspected the finished ones. We may believe the old account that said he worked day and night. Finally, the machines were completed and ready for setting up.

52

The Arkwright Equipment Reproduced

New England had many "clothier's shops," places where immigrants from England, skilled in textile work, would perform the various finishing processes needed to improve the rough-woven fabrics made in the various local homes. The clothier's shop of Ezekiel Carpenter, built some six years earlier, became famous because of its selection as the place in which to set up the completed Slater-Arkwright equipment. It was located on the "Old Forge Lot," along Sargeant's Trench, adjacent to the bridge across the Blackstone River. Ezekiel Carpenter had purchased lands on the western bank from Stephen Jenks, together with one-quarter of the dam and water-power rights from the falls.

Mature mechanics had obeyed young Slater when he told them what to build, and although Moses Brown, who was paying the bill, had been a bit anxious at times, he had not weakened. This rather amazing trust in a young man who was practically a stranger reveals Slater's ability to inspire the confidence of others, the same ability that had made William Slater trust his son's judgment when he was a boy in Belper, and shrewd Jedediah Strutt give the boy heavier and heavier responsibilities while he was an apprentice. Now, the swift waters of the intake to Carpenter's Clothier's Shop were either to confirm the confidence of mechanics and financier, or to brand Slater as another of the ill-informed men, or even impostors, who had promised so much and delivered so little to the introduction of cotton machinery in America. Thus far, Slater's confidence in himself had seemed perfect. Immediately, came difficulties that revealed him to be a very human young man after all.

As introduced by Slater, the carding of the cleaned cotton was done in several steps. Hand-fed into the breaker card, the cotton was supposed to come out as a thin fleece, which when rolled into a lap (like cotton batting) would go to the finisher card in which the mass of misaligned, infinitely fine fibres would eventually be transformed into a delicate sliver (Slyver), ready to be drawn out, twisted, and spun into yarn. In Slater's test this did not happen. Supposed to complete the final alignment of fibres as the teeth of the carder's cylinder dragged them forward against the stationary teeth of the top cards, the machine merely rolled them up into a mass of cotton that would not pass through. Matters were at a standstill for some time, and young Slater was distraught. In the Slater legend is the account of the young man leaning against the fireplace in the Wilkinson home, racking his mind for the answer, tears coursing his cheeks.

"Art thou sick, Samuel?" Mother Wilkinson asked.

"If I am frustrated in my carding machine, they will think me an impostor," he blurted out.

In his desperation Slater even told Sylvanus Brown that perhaps he should run away; it seemed the only way out. And the wise, older man gave the distressed younger one the needed advice.

"Have you seen one of these carders work in your own country?" Sylvanus asked.

"Yes!" Slater replied.

"Then it can be made to work here," the practical Sylvanus said.

So Slater and Brown continued their study of the defective cards that should turn out well-aligned fibres but did not.

While awaiting dinner at his home, Sylvanus picked up a pair of hand cards which his wife had been using to prepare cotton for her spinning wheel. Her husband studied the teeth of the hand cards: scores of bent wires, sloped at a definite angle. He noticed that they lay at a quite different angle from that of the thousands of teeth of the Slater carder that was not performing properly.

The solution is quickly told. Slater had correctly specified the bend of the teeth; it was merely that the poor leather of his machine cards had not held the teeth to this angle. After the thousands of teeth had been tediously bent to a proper angle with a scrap of old grindstone, the Slater carder worked. Already the water frame for spinning the carded cotton had been tried and found to work perfectly. Once again, young Slater was happy.

His period of intense discouragement had undoubtedly been a reaction from the terrific strain under which he had labored during the previous months. The answer did not come to Slater in a dream, as was told in a later, discredited legend. In Carpenter's shop, the first successful American cotton mill was now ready to start operation under the terms of the Almy, Brown & Slater agreement.

Today, we may examine two of the units of the Arkwright equipment made by Slater and set up in Carpenter's shop in 1790. One of the "carding engines" and a water-frame spinner are now on exhibit in the U. S. National Museum (Smithsonian) in Washington.

To those who know the history of the Slater-built Arkwright machines, they are among the most inspiring exhibits at Smithsonian. Like the early textile equipment on exhibit in

English museums, they are crude, and their working elements are far short of the smoothly efficient, functional arrangements by which modern equipment spins cotton into yarn for to-day's high standards. But it was the best American spinning gear of the time, and it made good yarn.

4

DURING THE YEAR when Slater had been building his reproductions of the Arkwright machines, events in the young United States of America had occurred that had seemed of great importance at the time. Rhode Island had finally ratified the Constitution, making unanimous the acceptance of this rule of government; the District of Columbia had been ceded to the United States by Maryland and Virginia; sad defeats and glorious victories had occurred in the bitter fights with the Indians who then threatened the areas that are now the states of Ohio and Indiana.

From today's perspective, however, the start of our first practical cotton mill by Slater on December 20, 1790, was the outstanding event of the year. He succeeded, where many others had failed, in the introduction of the textile machine methods that were to lead the way to the solution of the most difficult problem of the young American republic—its need of adequate industrial facilities to develop its great natural resources. Christmas came five days later, and we may be sure that the Wilkinson family celebrated his success to the full extent allowed by the strict regulations on worldly things by the Society of Friends to which they belonged.

Let us take time to examine the old records, in the light of the prime factors of any manufacturing venture: the kind of people who operated the Slater machines, the material handled, the machines used, and the power that drove them.

Children were the mill hands in America's first successful cotton mill, under the strict supervision of young Slater, now twenty-two years of age. The first record of employees begins with Monday, December 20, 1790, though some say that the new machinery began producing yarn as early as October. During the first week four boys, Turpin and Charles Arnold, Smith Wilkinson, and Jabez Jenks, were employed full time. On the next Monday (December 27) Eunice Arnold, on Wednesday of the same week Otis Borrows, and on Thursday John and Sylvanus (Varnus) Jenks commenced work. On the following Monday (January 3) Ann Arnold was added to the list, and during that week all the nine operatives, seven boys and two girls, worked the full time of six days. The same operatives also continued in the fourth week, though either "Varnus" Jenks or Smith Wilkinson (there is an error in the record which makes this point uncertain) worked only five days, while Turpin Arnold was absent two half-days.

All these workers were children of from seven to twelve, according to Smith Wilkinson, Slater's brother-in-law, who began work for Almy, Brown & Slater at the age of ten by tending the breaker. The juvenile character of Slater's force did not strike him as unusual. The English mills of Strutt, Arkwright, and others teemed with children, many of whom, sadly enough, were recruited from foundling asylums. Slater was fortunate in having better stock to draw upon in America.

Generations of American children had grown up in the atmosphere of home spinning and weaving of wool and linen, and more recently, to a small extent, the processing of cotton.

58

From early colonial times schools had been fostered, or even legally prescribed, for the training of children to spin. Unlike the harshly exploited pauper children of England, Slater's children had already received the rudimentary knowledge needed for the tasks that he would assign them.

Properly trained in the machine methods of factory regulations, they became good help, turning out superior yarn under the supervision of Slater, who began to have the reputation of being a strict boss. In the legend it is said that he would cane an occasional youngster who failed in his task—this with no hard feelings from the parents, for Samuel Slater was fair in his discipline.

Under Slater, the children learned how to spin cotton by machine. Cotton was still somewhat of a novelty in New England, except for its then quite important usage—for candle wicks. In the ripe cotton boll are thousands of tangled fibres of infinitesimal diameter, which, under the microscope, reveal a natural twist that aids the processing of them into yarn. As received in New England, the cotton came in bales, then averaging about two hundred and twenty-five pounds in weight, hand-picked of most of the seeds, but still needing further preparatory cleaning. At the start, Slater found the American cotton inferior, because of poor cleaning, so he used Surinam (Dutch Guiana) cotton. It was sent out to the local women of Pawtucket to clean on their flakes. These were corded racks on which the cotton was beaten with willow switches to make a light fluffy mass, free of hulls and other trash, which was returned to the mill for carding.

Slater soon accepted American cotton, for three years later Eli Whitney invented his cotton gin that could properly clean the short-staple, green-seed cotton of the southern hinterland regions, in quantities that were fabulous compared to those produced by the old hand-cleaning methods.

In the winter operation of his cotton mill, Slater encountered a difficulty that had not existed in the mills in which he had worked along the River Derwent, for the Derwent did not freeze. According to one old account, the water which drained from the lead mines on Cromford Moor, upstream from Belper, kept the river sufficiently warm to prevent it from freezing, and it is still true today that no trouble from freezing water occurs at the Belper cotton mills on the Derwent. Slater found that the waters of the Blackstone River did freeze. For two hours each morning, long before breakfast and with no one to help, he had to break off the ice that froze the water wheel of the mill, to enable it to revolve. It was believed by many that the physical ailments that shortened his life came from this bitter regimen carried on throughout the winter months of operation of his cotton mill.

At his warm home, Moses Brown considered the active operation of this mill he had financed. His reactions were varied. Slater made so much good yarn that Brown was afraid he would flood the market. "Thee will soon spin all my frames out," he said to his English protégé. But in a proud letter to the Secretary of the Treasury, Alexander Hamilton, Moses wrote that his mill had proved that "mills and machines may be erected in different places, in one year, to make all the cotton yarn that may be wanted in the United States."

Samuel Slater kept on. Obviously, they would soon have to expand. Pawtucket was still the best location because of its

60

water power, but Carpenter's shop was becoming cramped. Another mill, nearby, perhaps?

There was a personal problem for him to solve, first, however, pertaining to Hannah, the young daughter of Oziel Wilkinson.

5

WHILE WE DO not know exactly how much Samuel Slater paid Mother Wilkinson for his board and room while he was constructing the Arkwright machines in the shop on Quaker Lane, one old record includes a bill for his board at eight shillings a week. In the varying ratio of shillings to U. S. dollars of the period, locally, this could have been from $1.34 to $1.92. He paid, therefore, between one and two dollars a week out of his wage of $1.00 per day while on this job. He had inherited real estate and a nail store from his father in England, but the collection of rents and profits therefrom by an Englishman who had only recently arrived in America was a difficult procedure. Therefore, his small wage must have been, largely, his only means of support. He must wait for two years before his share of the profits from the Pawtucket mill, if any, were computed. He could be content, however, for there was Hannah, the attractive younger daughter of Oziel and Lydia Wilkinson. Hannah was sixteen years old.

The Wilkinsons were of old English stock, whose roots reached much further back than those of Slater's own ancestors. Their coat of arms was of ancient origin, and its crest, although much more modern, had been granted on September 18, 1615. Later, Lawrence Wilkinson had sided with King Charles I during the civil war of his day, and upon that ill-fated monarch's beheading, had been banished to New England. Lawrence Wilkinson established the American branch of the family about 1657 in Providence, where he was assigned "three acres of land, lying by the new field, beyond the great swamp." For several generations, the family was active in local affairs, and John Wilkinson, born in 1724 at Smithfield, had an iron-manufacturing shop on Mussey's Brook, at its juncture with the Blackstone River in Smithfield Township.

His son, Oziel Wilkinson, who was to become Slater's father-in-law, was born in 1744-45, was trained by his father in the arts of iron manufacture, and became a noted inventor. He removed to Pawtucket in the year of Samuel Slater's indenture, 1783, and became a leading figure in this center of the iron and machine manufacture in Rhode Island. He had an anchor mill, made nails and farm tools, and set up a slitting and rolling mill. He was, indeed, a skilled artificer in metals.

Moses Brown naturally would mention the talented Wilkinson family to Slater, when the young Englishman asked where he could find proficient iron workers to help him build his cotton machines. Brown also solved another problem for Slater—where to find a home in tiny Pawtucket, which had only a few homes to choose from. "The Wilkinsons are a large family, and they surely can find room for one more," was his advice.

The Wilkinson family was a large one, for besides Oziel and his wife there were three daughters and the sons: Abraham, Isaac, David, Daniel, and Smith.

Mother Lydia Wilkinson would have to be consulted first, of course; and with her consent, arrangements were made for

63

Slater to board with them. A delightful legend describes the introduction of the well-bred young Englishman, an Episcopalian, to the younger daughter of this Yankee-Quaker family.

He was pleased, of course, that he would now have a place to live in and eat his meals; more pleased that it was so near his workshop—just a few houses down Quaker Lane, in fact—but after all, these were minor points. The great advantage was that in this new country where there were so few mechanics, he was going to live with some of the best iron workers in New England. As he strode along the unpaved gravel road that led to the Wilkinson's house, he mused on how they could talk shop in the long evenings. He turned aside now and then to let a fast chaise rattle past him, and quickened his own pace to pass a slow, rumbling ox cart.

He knew there were young daughters of the family to whom he must be polite, but he prayed that feminine chatter would not interrupt too much, this evening, for he had truly important questions to ask forty-five-year-old father Oziel Wilkinson and his son David. So many of the machine parts had to be made of wood that the sturdiness of the few fastening metal parts became important. How reliable, for instance, would be the hand-forged and hand-threaded iron bolts? With their crude tools, how would Americans drill true holes to take the spindle shafts? Could their few welds of iron joints be counted upon? He frowned, as he realized that he must design, himself, the special tools required to make certain parts.

He awoke from his musings with a start. Before him was the house that had been pointed out as the place where these Wilkinsons lived. They are iron workers all right, he said to himself, appreciating the neatly shaped strap hinges and the

64

SLATER SPINNING FRAME, 1790

Original 48-spindle frame built by Samuel Slater in Pawtucket, Rhode Island, in 1790. The first spinning frame built by Slater was a 24-spindle frame, the second, this 48-spindle frame, pictured in the Textile Hall after renovation, January 1959. After the two spinning frames were withdrawn from actual service they were stored in the attic of the mill for many years. In 1856 a carding machine and the 48-spindle frame were presented to the Rhode Island Society for the Encouragement of Domestic Industry. In assembling the spinning frame several parts from the 24-spindle frame were used.

This frame was taken apart and reassembled many times during the past hundred years. A number of parts were lost and several incorrectly assembled. In 1958 the frame was restored as nearly as possible to its original condition. All replaced parts were so marked.

Neg. No. 45363. Courtesy of the Smithsonian Institution.

➤

cleverly formed grip and latch that guarded the wide front door through which he must enter. Through the narrow panes of a front window he imagined that he saw a flutter of calico, as he knocked lightly on the door. Mother Wilkinson opened the door and said: "Come in, Mr. Slater."

She stepped aside and he entered. And he saw her—young Hannah Wilkinson—and somehow, handmade bolts, welds, and special tools seemed the furthest thing from young Samuel Slater's mind.

Rather, he looked into the steady eyes of this girl. She was so sure that he did not see her, as she peered through the narrow opening of the back door through which she had fled on his approach, that she did not attempt to control the twinkle of her eyes and her appreciation of the build and countenance of this tall Englishman who her father had said would soon come.

Was she child or woman? He did not know. She revealed to him a sweet, feminine, ageless allure, and she was necessary to him, a normal young man, away from home, so intense in his concentration on his business mission that it took the miracle of the quick meeting of their eyes to swing him back to the masculine urgency of his need of her. Demurely, she dropped her eyes, noting that he had seen her; but she did not attempt to conceal her knowledge of his notice of her, and there was instantaneous understanding between Hannah Wilkinson and Samuel Slater.

Their courtship was the normal getting-acquainted period of a man and girl of different backgrounds. By the wide fireplace, in the light of the fluttering, cotton-wicked candles, he told her of the pleasant English countryside, now so often

65

spotted with tall factories; of splendid, yet squalid London; of the great ships of Liverpool, Bristol, and London. She told him of Indians who had destroyed Pawtucket in King Phillip's War, years back, and of its prompt rebuilding.

The comforting surcease from his hard program during the building of his Arkwright equipment gave the intense young man the needed respite to enable him to continue his work with renewed vigor.

There was the usual family concern about the difference of their religions. Surely, he could not expect them to countenance a marriage between a Friend and an Episcopalian, her parents admonished Slater. There came, then, two ultimatums. Because of the problem of religious difference, the Wilkinsons said that Hannah would be sent to a distant school, in the hope that she could forget her suitor.

"You may send her where you please, but I will follow her to the ends of the earth," was the ultimatum of Samuel Slater to the parents of his beloved. Young Slater's tenacity carried the day and they were married on October 2, 1791.

Thus goes the fine legend of the courtship of Samuel Slater and Hannah Wilkinson and its consummation in a marriage that proved to be a very happy one.

6

HANNAH WILKINSON SLATER was happy. She was proud of her tall husband who, despite his youth, was becoming a noted character in Pawtucket and elsewhere, for his keen ability in the practical machine processing of raw cotton into yarn of a superior quality. His business activities kept him long hours from home, but they soon set up housekeeping in a fine frame house built only a few rods from the Old Slater Mill, and he could spend more hours with her there. It was the first house Slater owned in America—two and one-half stories high, nicely clapboarded, and with a huge brick chimney in the center. Pictures of this now demolished house show it to have had the ample windows and the pleasing lines that go with early New England architecture.

Like all Yankee girls, Hannah was an accomplished seamstress. She had been well trained in the textile arts by her mother, who, in turn, had been trained by her mother; and so, back through generations the girls had been taught to work. They learned to spin, weave, and of course, to help make their own clothing since colonial time, when it is said every New England home was a textile factory.

Ten years before the Revolution, Governor Moore of New York reported: "Every house swarms with children, who are set to work as soon as they are able to spin and card." Thus, Hannah had inherited the art of spinning wool and flax, and

67

her natural ability enabled her to go a step further. We can imagine her smoothing the linen thread as she started to make Samuel a shirt from the firm fabric of the cotton cloth, home-woven from Slater-made yarn, of course.

Linen thread, made from flax, was universally used for sewing because of its strength, although it was rough. The smooth and even yarn spun by Slater from the long-staple Surinam cotton would make sewing easier, Hannah mused, if only it were strong enough. In this year, 1793, Hannah, who was about nineteen years old, found that two strands of the fine cotton yarn could be twisted by skillful manipulation on her spinning wheel into one thread that was stronger than the rougher linen threads.

Hannah had invented cotton sewing thread—two-ply No. 20 thread, as now designated by the trade! Her father and brothers were delighted, and in later-built Wilkinson mills they made cotton thread.

Her husband was proudest of all at Hannah's accomplishment. Yet he did not become enthusiastic in the development of machines to do what Hannah had done on her hand spinning wheel. It would be wrong to say that Samuel Slater, whose later career reveals many diverse interests, had a one-track mind. He had shown that he could make money in the production of superior cotton yarn for weaving. He must make more money to support his talented wife properly; he would stick to yarn for weaving. Long years later, a few years before his death and more years after Hannah had died, Slater established the Phoenix Thread Company, and he then complained that the demands of his agents for commissions kept the profits from the thread business very small. Perhaps, in his day, he felt that the thread business was an auxiliary that could wait a while for development.

At any rate, today's historians of textile processes credit Hannah Wilkinson Slater with the introduction in America of cotton thread, the manufacture of which is now such an important branch of the textile industry.

It is of more than passing interest to note that the Strutt and the Arkwright cotton mills, established on the River Derwent during Slater's time, are today component parts of a great English cotton trust. It is called the English Sewing Cotton Company, Ltd., and it makes superior cotton thread, just as Hannah Slater did more than a century and a half ago.

Double-spun twist yarn for hosiery was a product for which Slater did not have to devise special machines, as would have been the case if he had decided to start the manufacture of cotton sewing thread. Stocking yarn was an old product, in the making of which Slater had had excellent experience while an apprentice to Jedediah Strutt in Belper.

Years earlier, Strutt had made his start in the textile industry by his invention of a clever stocking frame. The then current yarns, spun by hand or on jennies, were too soft and loose for making good stockings, Strutt soon learned. As he developed his Arkwright spinning frames in Belper, he found that superior stocking yarn could be made on them if spun from two rovings instead of the single roving used for common cloth or calico. The resultant smooth, even yarn passed readily through the needles of the stocking frame, and one of the products for which the Strutt mills were most noted was their stocking yarn. Slater also became noted for his manufacture of this excellent product, which he introduced in America.

7

INTRIGUING LETTERS APPEAR in the dusty file of handwritten letters from Samuel Slater to his partners, dated from 1790 to 1793, during his operation of the cotton mill in Carpenter's shop. These letters complain of the delays of Almy & Brown in performing their part of the partnership agreement. Bluntly, he "needles" them, expressing his resentment at the poorly-cleaned cotton they bought him. They were also often behind in their shipments; they had not sent his reeler the pair of shoes they had promised and she could not come to work that day; and again and again he continues to complain of the shortage of cotton and of its poor quality, when they had finally sent him a shipment.

There were troubles with his equipment—alterations to the spindle shafts were needed, and Sylanus Brown "will neither alter them himself nor allow me to do it in his shop." . . . "A number of the frames are stopped for want of rollers." "Please give me a little advice concerning the candles, whether I shall leave off work every night or buy them by the pound here."

Smartly, he appealed to the one instinct his Yankee-Quaker partners should respond to: the fact that their delays were causing them to lose money—"Dec. 19, 1791: NB. I wish there might be a little more attention paid to this business at least we shall lose 13 or 14 dollars this week by shortness of

70

cotton." Samuel Slater was merely going through the stage of trying to cooperate with associates who just could not seem to keep up with his driving energy. Ultimately, there could be but one answer to such a situation—in any venture in which Samuel Slater was to engage, he should be boss, unhampered by associates who could not match his pace. Not quite yet, but soon, this was to be the goal of young Samuel Slater.

As time went on, Moses Brown came to admire the compelling energy of his young partner. Twenty years later, when the cotton business had become their greatest business, he wrote of Samuel Slater, "I should be pleased if my children could do, with their four, in part as he has done. Notice his energy and perseverance on the one hand in pushing to a successful establishment this great industry, and on the other, his moderation and prudence in management, etc."

Slater was getting results in his little cotton mill, and in America this was a novel situation. Among the few locations where men were attempting to spin cotton yarn by machinery, in little Pawtucket was one that was pre-eminently successful while others were destined to fail soon. It was outgrowing the small clothier's shop, which even with an anchor mill and a few other mills, did not begin to utilize the power that the Blackstone River could provide.

Like the proprietors of any successful small venture, Almy, Brown & Slater decided to expand. They constructed, in 1793, what is now the shrine of the American cotton industry: the Old Slater Mill. The site of the mill and the water-power rights had been purchased in 1791 by Moses Brown and Oziel Wilkinson for "350 Spanish milled dollars." It was bought from Cynthia Jenks as executrix of the will of Jonathan Jenks.

The story of this ambitious enterprise provides a typical example of early American water-power development—the arrangement of dam, millpond, flume, water wheel, tailrace and the mill itself.

Blithely ignoring the effects on the water-power rights of other users, Almy, Brown & Slater built a new dam, some twenty rods upstream of the dam at Carpenter's shop. As frequently occurred, when the fine balance of water-power rights was disturbed, years of litigation ensued, during which the Old Slater Mill continued operation, while the courts decided upon the riparian rights of the others who objected to the construction of this new dam.*

Dams across running rivers are hard to build, for somehow, the flow of the river has to be let by during construction. In the summer months when the flow is small, coffer dams are built to divert the flow to a narrow channel near a bank while the dam is built, and the channel is then closed by quick construction methods. Practical Oziel Wilkinson built the upper dam. It was undoubtedly an early form of rock-filled, timber-crib dam, the vestiges of which type occur throughout glacial New England where rocks are plentiful. That is, in the dry season, huge logs of wood were placed and bolted together crib fashion across the river bed. The cribs were then filled with large boulders, too heavy for the current to wash away. In this common, old method, the top of these rock-filled cribs was covered by a sloping plank floor, from a point upstream. Thus, the greater the impact of the river flow in high flood,

---

* See Note 5, Appendix A, pp. 186-87.

the more solid the dam became. Oziel complained about the poor plank furnished by Almy & Brown for this purpose.

Research indicates that the flume of the Old Slater Mill ran under the northeast corner of the building. Emerging from under the building, the water then flowed along the east wall beside which the water wheel was mounted. A Slater letter dated Nov. 23, 1793, reads: "Want abt thousand feet of pine boards to lay a floor on the floom under the building." Regarding the masonry-walled tailrace from water wheel to river, Slater wrote on October 19, 1793: "Eviliths are not able to get down any stones until rains come as the water too low for the Scow [even] to go up empty—I wish a mason may be procured timely so as to begin on the Arch as soon as possible the Stones are got down." Note that these letters are dated several months after the mill started operation.

Slater remembered the troubles from ice at Carpenter's, and demanded boards to enclose the water wheel on the east end of this, his first factory that kept most of the processes of making cotton yarn under one roof.

The water wheels then in use throughout the world were of three types: overshot wheels, over which the water flowed; undershot wheels, where the water would impinge against the lower floatboards; and breast wheels, where the water hit the wheel at about the level of the center of its horizontal shaft. The shallow flume at the Old Slater Mill leads us to surmise that the Old Mill was powered by a breast wheel.

The Old Mill had two and a half stories: it was a 44 x 30 foot building with walls, floors, and roof constructed wholly of wood. New England still had vast forests to clear, and timber was therefore plentiful, making wood the common material for construction, despite the great danger from fire. Slater realized the fire hazard, of course, and with good reason.

Undoubtedly, like other early English cotton mills, the 1776 Strutt mill in Belper, in which Slater had worked, had masonry walls on the exterior. Its floors, however, were of plank, supported by timber beams and posts. The early English mills were soon found to be great fire hazards, because of the wooden floors. With highly combustible cotton fibres in process, oil-drippings from the machines, candles for lighting, and the static electricity generated from belts, the danger from fire was ever imminent.*

Thus, viewed from the modern perspective attained by many decades of experience in fire preventive measures, Almy, Brown & Slater built a fire trap. Rigid rules to prevent fires were one of Slater's more important operating procedures. Only one fire in the Old Slater Mill is recorded, however, per a letter from him to Almy & Brown in the year 1811.

> N. Providence Oct. 9th 1811
>
> Messrs Almy & Brown,
> About 45 minutes past ten lst night, the disagreeable noise of a cry of fire, fire was again heard thro' the streets in this place, which was in our Spinning Room, when the people first got to the factory, the top frame over one of the spinning frames blazed fairly, but Joshua Vaughn & a few others broke the Sash in & with the help of Pales only, put the fire out before the Fire Engine got there I do think that the present alarming circumstance requires our immediate attention to,

---

* *See* Note 6, Appendix A, pp. 187-88.

the adoption of some method or other, that will in some measure contribute towards more effectually securing our property here & elswhere against fire—As respects the cause of the Fire. Many are of opinion it was set on fire wilfully, but I think & hope not.

> In haste Yrs etc.
> S. Slater

The old Slater Mill has been often enlarged and rebuilt during the one and a half centuries that have ensued since it was first constructed. Research in the records of the early mill, however, provides a reasonably accurate description of the original construction, which should interest modern builders of cotton mills.

Today, in the Old Slater Mill Museum occupying the Old Mill, the original posts and beams of the section built in 1793 may be seen in their original locations. The mill was of hybrid construction, resembling the stout New England barns in some details and the quaint old saltbox farmhouses in others. Like the barns, it had well-braced, exterior posts mortised and pegged to heavy cross beams from which smaller, hewn beams were attached to carry the plank floors. Like the farmhouses, the mill had clapboard on its exterior and whitewashed plaster on the interior. The sloping roof was supported on "A"-framed rafters.

The builders could have designed a better type of exterior wall, with insulating air space between plaster and outer boards. As it was, they built a cold shop. Slater wrote later (Nov. 14, 1793): "The children are quivering this morning at seeing it Snow and Cold and no Stoves."

During the long hours before full sunrise and after twilight, the mill was lighted by cotton-wicked candles.

The Old Slater Mill had a bell tower, with a bell that weighed sixty pounds, bought from Syprian Stery, a merchant of Providence. Whether they slept on feather beds or corn-husk mattresses, Pawtucket men, women, and children who worked for Slater must have come to dislike this bell. Long before daylight, above the roar of the falls at the dam, its clang would awaken them and tell them to arise and go to work.

When the Mill was finished the three carders and the two spinning frames totaling seventy-two spindles were taken from Carpenter's shop to the mill and placed in position. With the other necessary equipment set up, spinning began on July 12, 1793. The Old Slater Mill was a going concern.

On the grassy area about the old mill, women and children spread the spun yarn, praying for days of long-continued sunshine. They kept the yarn continuously wet, using watering pots; bleaching it under the action of the sun, the air, and the dew, until, after some four weeks, it was ready for weaving.

Samuel got a raise in pay. As superintendent of the mill he received $1.50 per day, in addition to his share of the profits.

The mill had been built at the expense of, and was owned by, Almy, Brown & Slater, the mill privilege (right to the water power) remaining the property of Moses Brown till 1801. Then Moses conveyed to William Almy and Obadiah Brown (who had replaced Smith Brown in the firm) "for love and affection," two-thirds, and to Samuel Slater, for a price, one-third of his interest of three-eighths of the mill privilege; and Thomas Arnold and Oziel Wilkinson each retained his interest. By the original agreement of 1790, Slater owned one-half of the mill and Almy & Brown one-half.

Shrewd bookkeeping was needed to keep the division of the profits straight between those who owned partial shares of the machinery and building and fractional parts of the valuable water-power rights shared with other mills on the swift Blackstone River that served them.

There were still available water-power rights on the Blackstone River, and across the river at the eastern end of the upper dam was room for still another cotton mill in the town of Rehoboth, Massachusetts (now a part of Pawtucket, Rhode Island). The possibility of another mill held an attraction to Slater, now in his mid-twenties.

III
The Mills
1801-1817

1

It was the year 1799, the end of the virile eighteenth century, during which the Industrial Revolution had made its start and was now in full swing in England. It was the tenth anniversary of the coming of Samuel Slater to America, and of his introduction of the textile processes of the Industrial Revolution in the United States. It was also the tenth anniversary of the young United States of America.

It had been a strenuous decade for Samuel Slater, and at its end he made an important decision. He decided to start a new textile venture in which he should have complete management.

We have noted his operating difficulties under an arrangement whereby his partners had control of the purchase of the raw materials. There was also their seemingly generous commission for marketing the finished yarn in addition to their share of the profits, though no squaring of accounts had been made for several years.

Buried in the bookkeeping records of Almy & Brown, who virtually had control of the financial part of the partnership, was Slater's share of the accumulated profits. Slater had written his partners demanding an accounting and practically threatening to stop operations while the unprocessed stock and the spun yarn could be computed; and in response Almy & Brown had deplored "so infamous a measure."

This definite dissension between Slater and Almy & Brown was not at all alleviated by a subsequent move of Slater's partners which occurred in this year, 1799.

Spurred by the success of Almy, Brown & Slater, a small outfit called the Warwick Spinning Mill had started yarn manufacture. This mill was located in that part of the old town of Warwick now known as Centerville, a few miles south of Pawtucket. Finding that more money to finance their business was needed, its proprietors had sold one-half interest in the business to William Almy and Obadiah Brown, who took control on August 1, 1799. It was a peculiar situation to the young Englishman: the two Quakers entering into a business that was in competition with the Old Mill, which they jointly ran with him their partner! He was justifiably angry, and became highly indignant when they sent the mechanic of the Warwick mill, John Allen, to the Old Slater Mill to study and measure the improved devices which Slater had set up there.

When Allen refused to desist in his measurements, Slater threatened to throw him out of the window and proceeded to start doing so; then tactful Obadiah Brown took the measuring rule and said: "I will finish the work and see if Samuel will serve me as he did thee." This from his friend Obadiah! In spite of Slater's anger, the measurements were taken and the Warwick spinning mill was successful for many years.

This period of dissension did not prove disastrous in the future relationship of the shrewd Yankee-Quakers and the young Englishman who by this time had developed a business

82

shrewdness equal to theirs. For years Almy, Brown & Slater continued to operate the Old Mill and at least one other Slater venture. Slater also used Almy & Brown as merchants to supply materials to build his Webster mills, its Slater & Tiffany account running into several thousand dollars.

Further evidence of mutual friendship and respect was shown when, in making his will, Obadiah Brown appointed Slater as executor of his estate; and Slater also continued to be a friend of Moses Brown to the end of his life.

The Warwick episode, however, served one purpose. It kindled the long-smouldering coals of discontent; and Slater's determination to start on his own was clinched by that move of Almy & Brown's; a similar move on his part would be only in retaliation for what they had done.

Slater had a one-half interest in the Old Mill; he also had the means to start another one, this time with partners whom he could understand better, and with himself as senior partner. The proper site for his proposed venture was obvious: on the east end of the upper dam, in Rehoboth. The group that purchased this site from David Kennedy on November 11, 1797, consisted of Moses Brown, Thomas Arnold, Oziel Wilkinson, and Samuel Slater. Kennedy's interest in the upper dam and the right to one-half the water power was included in this deal. The group, with the exception of Slater, now had full right to the entire water power at the upper dam. Perhaps Slater's plan to start a mill independently was not known at the time to Moses Brown, whose main object in entering into the arrangement was, apparently, to obtain ownership in the complete water-power rights of the location.

When Slater's intentions to start a new mill of his own on the east bank became known, his Almy and Brown partners refused him permission to utilize the water power at the site, and Slater applied to the courts for a division of the land and water-power rights between them. The jury reported in his favor and the court approved his appeal at its next session.

The firm of Samuel Slater & Co., founded in 1798, was made up, besides him, of Oziel Wilkinson, Timothy Green, and William Wilkinson, the two latter, as well as Samuel, having married daughters of Oziel Wilkinson. By the court's decision, Slater, holding a one-half interest in the company, and the members of the Wilkinson family the other, were given full control of the land and their share of the water-power rights, and construction immediately began on a wooden building— nearly a duplicate of the Old Mill. It was completed in 1801, and for the simple reason that it was painted white, became known as the White Mill.

The White Mill was the first mill with the Arkwright system to be erected in Massachusetts. At the session of the Massachusetts Legislature in June 1799, "on the petition of Samuel Slater, stating his intention to establish a cotton mill in Rehoboth," an Act was passed on June 22, providing "that all buildings that may be erected in said town for the purpose of a cotton mill, together with the materials and stock employed in the manufacture of cotton, be, and the same are hereby exempted from taxes of every kind, during the term of seven years from the first day of April next."

Soon after the White Mill started operations, a disturbing situation confronted Slater. He had a walk-out on his hands; he was deserted by some of the men whom he had trained in the Arkwright methods and who had noted the air of prosperity that prevailed in mills managed by him. There is money to be made in the cotton business, they said to one another, if only we could find someone to put up the money. Quickly these men found backers. In 1797, Elisha Waterman of Cumberland, Rhode Island, and Benjamin Walcott of Seekonk had purchased property in Abbot's Run, a tributary of the Blackstone River. They had built a dam at Robbins Hollow here and set up a fulling mill (later called Cumberland Mills) that would cleanse wool fabric of its grease and finish it. As in the case of the Warwick Spinning Mill, its proprietors, observing the success of two cotton mills in Pawtucket, decided to branch out into the cotton business. It had a good location as to water power and now, with the Slater deserters as operatives, the mill started operations in the year 1802.

It was an early application of the formula whereby, within a half-century, New England was spotted with scores of cotton mills. In the earlier period, before steam power was found to be practicable, the factors of the formula were: first, adequate water power; second, capital for financing, and last, experienced men for operatives.

We may be sure that Slater (perhaps from an upper window in the White Mill) observed his departing operatives on parade; and reviewed with mixed emotions a procession of jubilant Yankees celebrating their independence, each marcher wearing a skein of cotton around his hat. There was much noise and confusion and a few spectators had to pull tightly on their horses' reins to avoid runaways as the beasts quivered nervously at the shouts. Slater may have admired the courage of these men he had trained; he wished them success in their venture somewhat ruefully; on the other hand, he admonished them that while the reward for their determination might possibly be great, they must expect many difficulties in the tricky business of spinning.

The White Mill was operated under the firm name of Samuel Slater & Company—at the age of thirty-three Slater had "arrived." He needed the talents of his partners in operating matters, and perhaps their financial backing, but he was the senior partner who had the last words in matters of decision. In *The United States Chronicle* of July 30, 1801, appeared the announcement of the mill's ability to make all kinds of yarn for "warp, filling, two-and-three-thread stocking yarn, suitable for weaving and knitting, whitened or brown, wholesale or retail, at a short notice . . . equal, if not superior, to any manufactured in America."

About this time, William Almy wrote Moses Brown, telling him of a proposed change in the Almy, Brown & Slater agreement. Under the proposed new arrangement "Samuel" was to receive one-third mill privileges, although he had received one-half by the earlier agreement. Slater was then in poor health, and it was suggested that he needed an assistant supervisor. Slater reluctantly signed the revised agreement. There was this much in his favor: the White Mill venture was under way and promising good returns and he had an assistant at the Old Mill. With this he had to be satisfied—anything to get along with these Quaker associates.

2

SLATER, WHO WAS PROUD of his apprentice years, first sought out Rhode Island children who would serve in the same capacity. It was a sign of the times that he was unsuccessful. Radical changes in the standard of living in Pawtucket, Providence, and the adjacent villages were taking place; prime factors in these were Slater's increasing production and a ready market. In fact, a whole new social class was evolving: that of the textile mill hand.

The first mill hands were mostly children whose parents had become too independent to allow their boys and girls to serve as apprentices but were willing for them to live at home and work in the mill, frequently working along with them, though of course only at adult tasks.

It was several years before Slater included power weaving in his operations, and the hand looms which had provided fabric for the family clothing for years were still kept busy by those to whom the spun yarn was "let out" for weaving at home.

Slater is not credited with the introduction of the power looms in the American cotton mills, but when they did come into use in a few years, a new type of mill hand appeared: the adult loom-tender.

Before Slater's industry was started southern New England was predominantly an agricultural community, and with little cash income, each family had to be self-supporting. They cultivated their little fields for vegetables and meal, slaughtered an occasional cow, pig, or sheep for meat, and made their clothing from wool sheared from their own sheep.

There was little money for the finer things of life when such a large percentage of trading was done by barter. A cash income of $100.00 was a princely sum for a family, and not many farmers could buy the better, imported fabrics for clothing, or afford to send their children to the few existing schools. Yet the farmers of New England were an independent lot; each perforce was a jack-of-all-trades, but they were versatile, and having an aptitude for the new spinning processes Slater taught them, provided, with the womenfolk and children, efficient mill hands for him and other mill operators. As Slater's business increased and he reached farther and farther out to find mill hands, these farmers found that many days' work in the factory could be fitted in with their own routine, and as a result a greater degree of prosperity came to these families in the farming areas adjacent to Pawtucket.

A novel situation arose soon, quite different from that which had existed back in England for generations before the coming of the machine spinners. Then, it was unusual to find sufficient hand wheel-spinners to keep the hand weavers occupied, and it was a common saying that eight spinners were needed to keep one weaver busy. Now, in Pawtucket, with the weaving still to be done by hand, the machine spinning frames were producing so much yarn that it was difficult to find sufficient weavers to make it into cloth. Experienced weavers were sought from far away places, and the immigrant weavers from England were a good source of supply. Most of these became

88

good citizens as well as proficient weavers on the hand loom, but others were not careful in their ways of living, and their actions contributed to the serious prejudice against textile mill hands that continued for several years respecting both the immigrants and certain American mill hands of dissolute character with whom they caroused.

Not everyone felt this prejudice. Many thoughtful American citizens realized that only determined men could stand the hardships through which the immigrants went to reach this country; they respected them for their courage and were fair in their distinction between the good and the bad. A good representative anecdote illustrating the latter disposition and based on historical records of the period is of an American couple riding in their chaise one day, near Providence.

The chaise was both sturdy and light. It was well adapted to the rough gravel turnpike heading westerly from Providence. As its two wheels encountered a "thank-ye-marm," the ash poles that extended from whiffletree base to rear strut transferred the jolt to the elastic, leather springs that carried the body, which would float up and down in a graceful undulation, to which the two passengers soon became accustomed. In the summer one could average five miles an hour in a chaise. On a day in early spring, however, it was prudent to go slow; the soft roadbed had many hidden boulders which caused hard jolts, and one had to brace against the floor board or side rail. In all seasons, it was pleasant to stop for an occasional breathing spell, so that horse and passengers might rest.

The last stop had been at the toll gate, some five miles back, and the driver decided it was time for a rest. He pulled up to one side and halted. As they rested, his wife spied two travelers in the distance, headed toward Providence. They walked briskly, although one stooped slightly under a burden resting on his shoulders. Coming opposite the chaise the way-farers stopped, and the woman in the chaise frowned as she studied them. Knee breeches and cloaks were of a different cut and fabric from those of Rhode Islanders; of good ma-terial, but worn. The taller of the two eased his burden, a small leather-bound trunk, to the ground. As he spoke to his companion, the woman recognized his dialect, and turned to her husband, whispering in disgust, "English mill hands! And they let mill hands off from paying the turnpike toll, just like other folks on foot don't have to pay if they're going to a funeral, or to church, or to town meeting."

Her husband wrapped the reins around the whip socket and turned toward the men on the road. "Mill hands can be good or bad," he muttered to his wife. "Let's hope these two are good ones." He smiled slightly as the man carrying the trunk addressed him.

"We're from Derbyshire, sir," the man said respectfully, "and would you be so kind as to tell us the way to Slater's Mill?"

At this, the smile of the chaise driver broadened. "You don't have to tell us where you're from," he answered. "We're pretty used to your lingo here, what with all you Britishers coming lately from Derbyshire, Lancaster, and Yorkshire. There's not much difference in the way men from any of the English textile towns talk. And as for Slater's, you've a long walk ahead. Five miles to Providence, and you'll know by the better road when you're there. For the turnpike stops at the

90

town line, and the town mends its roads better than the turn-pike corporation does, even if it did charge us twenty cents at the gate a few miles back. It'll be about three miles to Paw-tucket, where Slater's is, then."

The Englishman merely said, "Thank'ee," and turned to stroke the sleek neck of the horse.

At this gesture, the chaise driver became more friendly, and asked, "But why are you on the post-road turnpike that comes from New York? Don't tell me you've walked clear from there with your trunk."

"Indeed we did, sir," was the proud reply from the shorter man. "And, being good weavers from Derby Borough, we've made a pretty penny in the weeks we've been traveling, stop-ping for weaving jobs at the villages along the way. It was at one of those places we heard about Slater's, for they gave us Slater yarn to weave." He continued even more proudly, "It's good yarn I like, being a spinner as well as a weaver, and they did say Slater's is looking for both. So here we are." As it was his turn to carry the trunk, he picked it up and the two stepped out smartly for Providence.

Unwrapping his reins from the whip socket, the chaise driver drew them in and clucked to his horse. As the chaise rattled westerly, he turned to his wife and said: "Somehow I'm betting on those two. They're not riffraff, like some im-migrants, upsetting a town with their carousing. Slater seems to pick up good help, and he maintains good discipline. And he's started a Sunday School for the youngsters who work for him, which he didn't have to do, you know."

Slater badly needed more help; the Derbyshire man was right about that. The Old Mill of Almy, Brown & Slater, and the White Mill of Samuel Slater & Company spun so much yarn that the local home weavers could not keep up. Slater had to secure weavers from wherever they could be found; some came from American localities as far distant as Nantucket.

A few years later, at the start of the War of 1812 with Great Britain, figures became available that told of the influx of immigrant textile workers to America. Within three weeks after the declaration of war the State Department ordered all alien immigrants over fourteen years old to register, giving their occupation among other data required. Many trades appeared in the lists: textile workers, blacksmiths, whitesmiths, tanners, shoemakers, watchmakers; those who made gun barrels, cutlery, and other goods. Textile workers represented the largest occupational group in the lists of the states of Delaware, New Jersey, Rhode Island, and Pennsylvania.

A powerful incentive which induced men to leave England was the alluring picture of the advantages in this country painted in the letters written to relatives by those who had made the change successfully, Slater's relatives included. Anxious to benefit by his brother John's experience in a new and better machine spinning instrument, the Crompton mule, Slater sent for him. A niece, Mary, came of her own accord.

The textile industry in America owes much of its start to the experienced talent from the textile centers of Great Britain, and the Slater mills got their share. Slater's reputation for fair dealing made his mills a Mecca for mechanics and operatives at home and abroad.

Immigrants meet difficult problems in a new country, both social and financial. Slater is said to have helped thousands with proper advice and money. What better arrangement for him could there be for a man of his nature, than to assist those of his native country who worked faithfully for him, since loyalty, together with the ability to render him competent service, seems to have been the measure of how much he could help them solve their problems? Today we would call the Slater organization a paternal group, with the power to make decisions resting in its creator who had an old-fashioned interest in the family affairs of those who worked for him. To him this seemed to be as much a matter of good business policy as was his start of the Sunday School for his juvenile mill hands.

It was a fine summer Sunday morning, and a group of boys were planning how to spend it, their recreation being important after the long week in the Old Mill under the strict supervision of Samuel Slater. "Let's go to . . . Arnold's orchard," someone suggested, "there's good apples there." One boy, Nathaniel Dexter, who told the story later in life, demurred. He hadn't been brought up to steal apples or anything else, and Sunday stealing was particularly bad, according to Nathaniel.

Of course their boss, Samuel Slater, would happen to stop by just then, and the boys had to tell him of their argument. "I will propose something better than that," Slater said. "You boys come into my house and I will give you all the apples you can eat, and I will keep a Sunday School." Thus runs the story of the start of the first Sunday School in America, according to some authorities; certainly one of the first, according to others.

In 1790, little Pawtucket had neither church nor school, and Slater knew too much about the ignorance of so many English children who had worked in some of the cotton mills to want such a condition to exist in his mills. Strutt and Arkwright had taken remedial steps in England and the necessity to follow their example and provide a school for his juvenile hands had long been under Slater's consideration, so his invitation to the boys that Sunday was not the result of an offhand decision.

The long work-week left no day except Sunday for lessons of any kind, but the new school was not strictly one for religious study. It was created primarily to provide the children whose parents could not afford to send them to schools away from Pawtucket with a proper training in reading, writing, and arithmetic. Its first textbooks were five Webster spelling books, and the library consisted of three New Testaments. The fact that he was censured by the townspeople of Pawtucket for what they termed "profaning the Sabbath" did not hinder Slater for a moment, for with characteristic determination, once he had made up his mind that a course of action was right, he went right ahead.

For some time Samuel Slater taught the school himself, and it was very popular. Later, in 1796, the President of Providence College (later Brown University) told William Collier, a student there, that Samuel Slater had asked for someone who attended the college to teach the Slater School at a suitable salary. At first Collier declined, believing it improper to teach secular subjects on the Sabbath, but the wise president persuaded him that the instruction of boys was a most important service, and Collier accepted the assignment.

94

Several years later David Benedict, a student at the college and a Baptist minister, became the teacher of the Slater school. Benedict added Bible reading and religious instruction in the school. These teachers were paid for their services by Slater and his partners, according to the records of Almy, Brown & Slater, and also by Oziel Wilkinson.

Finally, the school was divided between the Baptist Church, of which Benedict was pastor, and St. Paul's Episcopal Church. Ultimately, in addition to the Sunday schools, day schools were started for children in all the mills in which Slater was interested, in some cases with Slater paying the full salaries of the teachers.

Samuel Slater and his business associates took the education of the young very seriously, as is evidenced by an abstract from the minutes of "The Proprieters of the Pawtucket School House" of which Slater was one of the original thirty-nine subscribers, when this organization was started in the year 1796:

> Where As the Instruction of Youth Hath in All Ages and Places been Esteemed the Greatest Blessing which God hath given to Mankind to bestow on their offspring and the Acquisition of Knowledge is that which above all other things Cultivates the Human mind Reforming and Correcting the Original barbarity thereof and Plaseing those who are Possessed of its Beautys as much above the Savages as the Savages are Superior to the Beasts *** And where as for that purpose it hath ever been found Advantagious and Necessary to Erect Proper Seminaries for Planting in Tender minds the Seeds of Virtue and Morality and for the Improvement of their Capacities so as to become Useful and Ornamental Members of Society—Strongly Impressed

with a Sence of Our Privileges and Duty in these Respects to our Selves our Offspring and Fellow Creatures —wee whose names are Hereunto Subscribed do Promis and Engage Each one for himself to the others that we will at our joint Expence Erect a House for the Purpose aforesaid***"

3

THE TEMPO OF LIFE in 1803 allowed people the opportunity to enjoy many things for which today they think they cannot spare the time. The combined village store and post office was a place for social visits; the incoming stage was of great interest and also broke the routine, and the wharf, when a boat docked, was a busy place for those whose only interest was to see what was going on as well as for those who had business there. The wharf at Providence was no exception. The packet from New York had just put in and passengers and cargo alike were being unloaded.

William Wilkinson was among those people who stood on the wharf watching with keen interest. His attention was caught by a tall young man who descended from the gang-plank and stood looking about him with a hesitancy that marked him for a stranger. Noting the young man's uncertainty, Wilkinson approached him.

"A safe ending to your journey, I see," he said.

"Aye," the man answered. "Except that I am not yet at the end of it. From Liverpool to New York—aye, a long, uncomfortable journey; from New York to here, and now, I have yet to get to a place called Pawtucket. Maybe you can tell me the procedure to take to get there. I have relatives there."

Wilkinson was eyeing him carefully. There was something familiar about the man—his speech and his general appearance; he reminded Wilkinson of someone.

"Thee'll be English, I take it," he said; and at the other's nod he added, "thee has relatives in Pawtucket?"

"Aye, my brother; his name is Samuel Slater."

We may imagine his surprise when Wilkinson introduced himself as also being a brother—by marriage—to Samuel Slater, as well as being a business partner.

"Providence has indeed smiled on me," the Englishman said as the two men shook hands. "I am John Slater."

Wilkinson caught the humor, and the twinkle in the other's eyes which he had so often seen in his brother's. He decided then and there to have a little fun at Samuel's expense. He would take this young brother to Pawtucket but would not tell Samuel who he was. John fell in readily with the idea.

"But first," Wilkinson said, "come to my house and refresh yourself after your long journey."

John gratefully accepted, well pleased with this evidence of kindness on the part of his brother's associate. He found that the ride to Pawtucket was only a matter of four miles or so and the two were soon on their way.

He admired the tall spruce and pines that lined the road in a profusion that did not exist in his sparsely-wooded country, a fact which would account for the difference in the construction of the houses they passed; he was used to homes of stone and brick. He noted, too, the lack of meticulously-trimmed hedgerows; what fences he saw were made of wooden poles. Although the chaise rolled easily along the road, he could

98

see that the roadbed did not compare with the smooth-surfaced Telford pavements now coming into use at home.

Wilkinson, noting his obvious interest, said, "It will be a strange country to you."

"Aye," John said, "it looks different to be sure."

Wilkinson was glad, as all Americans are, to show him the beauties of the countryside and to point out the things which he thought would have a particular interest for this man who was as much of a mill man as his brother. Samuel had told him about John.

Their pace was not fast and Wilkinson took the opportunity to tell John a little about Samuel's success in his cotton ventures.   89790

He cautioned John not to let Samuel know that he mentioned it to him, knowing that it would possibly provoke him to anger. Samuel was sometimes severe in his expression. He was always silent with regard to his business, and disliked it when the men spoke of where he was going or of what he was about; he also disliked anyone who was inquisitive or prying about his affairs; and he never interfered with other people's matters. Once some of his men had mentioned in the village that Mr. Slater was going to Boston next morning. He had found out about it and had gone to the mill in much anger at them.

Wilkinson spoke mostly of family affairs to John. It had been a trying time for Samuel Slater. True, his business ventures, particularly since he had branched out and taken charge as the senior partner, had been successful, and already it would seem that everything that came to his mill would be grist, as the saying went. Nevertheless, he had had cares, worries, and sorrows.

He and Hannah had been married several years before their first child was born. This had been a boy whom they had named William, probably for Samuel's father. Their first daughter, Elizabeth, had been born in 1798, two years later, and Mary had been born September 28, 1801. Their joy at her birth had been saddened by the death of William, in January of that same year. The two little girls had also died in infancy, and Samuel Jr., born on his sister Mary's birthday in 1802, was the only one of Samuel's children whom John would be able to see.

Wilkinson went on to tell John what a good husband and father his brother was, but this was no news to John. The family ties had always been close. William had just finished telling John of the schools which Samuel had established for the benefit of his young mill hands, John marveling at the extent of the advantage these youngsters had in working conditions over those of the English children, when the chaise drew up in front of Samuel's house.

Wilkinson pulled a straight face as Samuel came to greet them. "I have brought one of your countrymen to see you. Can you find anything for him to do?"

Of course, Slater greeted the Englishman kindly, for that was his custom. He would always ask questions of anyone who knew about textile matters—one of the ways he kept up-to-date on conditions in England.

"I would say you were from Derbyshire, from your accent," he said cordially.

100

John nodded. "Aye," he said, "from Belper."

Samuel became even more cordial. "I am acquainted with Belper," he answered, "and your name, sir?"

"John Slater," was the proud answer.

We may imagine the smile that had broadened John's face during the cross-examination by his older brother.

It is easy to understand Samuel's failure to recognize him; John had grown from a boy of thirteen to a tall young man of twenty-seven since Samuel had seen him.

Afterwards, William Wilkinson told of the scene when the two brothers were reunited in a David and Benjamin meeting. Question followed question, sometimes with no pause for an answer.

"Is my mother yet alive? How are my brothers and sisters? You must meet my sweet young wife, Hannah, and my son— Hannah, you will fetch the boy that he may kiss his Uncle John! How is my old master, Strutt? How is my old schoolmaster, Jackson? How faithfully he has given me news and told me of conditions at home. How is the old Holly House farm getting along? I have to be interested as a farmer since that is the way I got to America, you know." There was a general laugh as Samuel recounted his experiences as a "farmer" on his journey.

Wilkinson, who had thoroughly enjoyed the meeting of the two brothers, had been impressed by their deep affection for each other. Possibly this warmth was what inspired people's confidence in his brother-in-law. Wilkinson had left the two deep in conversation about mills. There was much Slater wanted to know, although even with the limited means of communication a century and a half ago, he had kept abreast of the improvements in English textile manufacturing.

At the time Slater built the one successful cotton mill in America (1790), England and Wales had one hundred and fifty water-frame factories and several factories with Hargreave jennies. In an industry of this scope, many defects of the crude early apparatus had been corrected by mechanics clever enough to devise better methods for the spinning of cotton yarn.

The coarse yarn made by jenny or water frame was sufficient for weaving strong goods: "thicksetts, velveteens, fancy cords and calico," but only the deft fingers of men or women could spin yarn suitable for the fine muslins that the French, Saxons, and Swiss sold in the English market for milady's voluminous petticoats and milord's fancy beruffled shirts. It was irksome to the English textile firms, with their marvelous machine spinners, to have to admit that this profitable product, muslin, was beyond the power of their machines to produce.

Years earlier (1779) the Englishman Samuel Crompton had conceived and developed a spinner that when perfected was to overcome this disadvantage. This was the Crompton mule, which was a hybrid combination of jenny and water frame. Fed to the rollers from creels at the back, the yarn continued to the spindles that were mounted on a carriage, which by clever controlling devices drew out the yarn at the time the rollers were stopped from turning, and then, as the carriage rolled back, wound the fine, strong yarn on the bobbins, ready for the finishing processes en route to the looms. As far as yarn was concerned, the machine had eventually beaten manual operations when Crompton mules were finally

102

set up and put to work in the cotton factories of England (1790). With mule spinning, England could make as fine and strong yarn as that produced by European hand-method competition.

For a short period England produced finished muslin cheaper, even with her weavers receiving thirty shillings per week, than her European competitors. To the chagrin of the English, however, the Europeans soon found that they could undersell England if they bought English mule-spun yarn and with their much lower paid hand weavers, wove it into muslin. This continued until Cartwright corrected the situation with his power loom.

The introduction of the Crompton mule was an outstanding landmark in the advance of machine methods in England. There it was the last word in cotton spinning, and Samuel Slater was determined to introduce it in America. His main objective in inviting his brother had been to secure information on the mule, obtained by John in the textile centers of Oldham and Manchester.

Immediately John Slater went to work for Almy, Brown & Slater. First, he had to become acquainted with American ways of making machines with the limited tools available, of far less advanced design than in his homeland. He had also to learn how to control the independent, rough and occasionally convivial mill hands in the new cotton industry, who were already giving Pawtucket a bad name among pious folks.

Because of its bad reputation, the young American cotton industry found it difficult to get suitable help, and sturdy folk from the farm areas were in demand. Overseers of Slater and other mills visited outlying farm sections to engage farmers' sons and daughters who, if as industrious as the Howland family of seven (who worked for Slater), might earn nearly $2.00 per day, when the whole family worked. These wages were usually paid in commodities like groceries, clothing, and rum, from the company stores of the mill owners. Although a firm might have ample capital, ready money for the payroll was difficult to obtain in this period of money scarcity, whereas the store commodities could be bought on time by the mill owner. The company store was the answer. A three-story brick building near the Old Mill was the store of Almy, Brown & Slater at this time.

It was during this period that Slater decided to expand once more. This, the most ambitious of any of his ventures, involved building another mill, and with this deviation from ordinary practice: to facilitate getting help, he decided to take the mill to the farm areas, rather than try to tempt the farm help to come to one built in a suburban area. Possibly he may have felt that such a move would eliminate, in part, the type of mill hand with which he had had so much trouble.

Obviously, a mill site farther up the Blackstone River that had served him so well would be best, and he sent John to find it. That he selected John shows his confidence in his younger brother, because this was a task which Slater could assign only to someone in whose judgment he could put complete trust.

John had spent a three-year training period in Pawtucket during which he had learned American machine methods and the Almy, Brown & Slater ways of getting results from people who worked for them. He had also learned that his brother had acquired the name of being a stern disciplinarian, albeit a fair man to work for. The trial period must have been successful, because to the various machine-minded Wilkinson "in-laws" Samuel added John as a member of the team that was developing his ever-expanding ventures.

By pack-horse trails along the Blackstone, John traveled from Pawtucket in search of a mill site. Soon, he was in the wilderness of northern Rhode Island, where, he could tell from experience, a dam could be built. By night he had to get used to the howl of an occasional wolf, the clamor of barking foxes and hooting owls. If he had thought he was in a strange country, en route to Pawtucket with Wilkinson, he was now doubly sure of it. By day, he reined in his horse and studied a promising vista that would combine the advantages of a desirable dam site with the level areas needed for a mill and other structures.

On the Monhegan (now the Branch) River, a tributary of the Blackstone south of the borderline of Rhode Island and Massachusetts and around twelve miles from Pawtucket, John found an ideal site, with a fall of about forty feet and ponds upstream forming natural reservoirs, thus providing ample water in all seasons. Well pleased with his find he returned to describe it to Samuel and the others; they were as well pleased, Samuel more so probably, because John had come through in true Slater fashion. Immediately William Almy and Obadiah Brown began the purchase of the land with the right to build a dam, and by 1806 had increased their holdings to a total of one hundred and twenty-two acres.

A new partnership was now formed, and Samuel, true to his custom, saw to it that John was rewarded for his good work. He made him a partner in this new firm designated as

Almy, Brown & Slaters, in which each of the four partners had equal ownership. The construction of the new venture was soon started.

The firm constructed the dam, canal, water wheel, tailrace, machine shop, and cotton mill, and Samuel made John the superintendent over the new mill.

Around this unit a small village soon grew. There were houses for mill hands to live in after their long days of labor. There were lots laid out for a church, a burying ground, a school, and a parsonage, and it became, in all respects, a typical, pleasant, New England mill town.

There is no way of knowing if Samuel Slater had quietly planned what followed. He always laid plans in a methodical way and the eventual outcome of this one may have entered his mind, although since he was a very modest man, it is doubtful. At any rate, in the month of May 1806, this village whose nucleus was the Slater mill, was incorporated into a town in its own right, distinct from Smithfield, of which it had formerly been a part; and was called Slatersville.

Modern Slatersville is an attractive town situated along the Branch River. Its textile mill is no longer in operation, but the vestiges of the foundations of the original mill are still in sturdy condition. Samuel Slater built things to last—from the foundation of a mill to the foundation of an enterprise. The most striking structure is the 1826 mill, a long, four-story masonry building with a tall bell-tower, also of stone. This was built when the earlier mill was burned down—a substantial loss. Two three and a half-story buildings face the mill across the highway; one still referred to as the Company Store, built in or about the year 1815. These buildings have a brick frontage with stone ends. Also facing the highway is a handsome wooden building which was built in 1815—the John Slater Mansion.

Slatersville stands today as a living memorial to a man's ambition, his perseverance, his honor, and his credit.

4

By happy circumstance, Samuel Slater had come to New England to start his American career in machine spinning. It was not by chance, however, that the new cotton industry made its greatest advance in New England, during its early period of promotion. The region had particular advantages, because of its location, geology, climate, and financial resources.

The beds of most of the rivers of New England slope steeply from source to mouth, providing the fall requisite to suitable water-power sites. In the day of poor roads, a river, in many instances, made the seacoast ports more accessible by providing an easy avenue of transport. Also, the clear water of the New England rivers was more suitable for bleaching the spun yarn than that of many other American localities.

The glacial gravel of the rocky hillside farms of New England was not conducive to farming as a means of livelihood; the farms produced little beyond the immediate needs of the farmers and their families, who were glad to supplement their scant earnings from agriculture with additional work as hands in the new cotton mills.

Since these were the days before humidifying apparatus appeared in these cotton mills, New England's favorable degree of humidity was a distinct advantage.

108

In its maritime cities, such as Boston, Salem, Portsmouth, and Portland, were shrewd financiers whose wealth had come largely from their courageous backing of the Yankee ships that sailed to the distant corners of the earth with American goods. It was, however, a risky business, bringing great profit in the case of a safe journey or none at all when the ship failed to return. Money invested in the promising cotton industry seemed to have a better chance of making a more predictable profit in good Yankee dollars, and since this was what these financiers were looking for, they decided to invest in a cotton-mill venture or two.

Mass production, in the form of bales or hanks of good cotton yarn, was introduced to New England by Samuel Slater and his competitors. The quantities produced were so great that some people could not imagine where it would find a market. This was illustrated by the experience of James Beaumont, when he proudly displayed his clever spinning machines to visitors at his new mill in Canton, Massachusetts. They were amazed—not at the machines, but at the huge quantity of yarn that they were turning out. "What on earth are you going to do with all this yarn? You never will be able to sell it in this vast world!" a woman visitor exclaimed.

Cotton yarn was becoming popular in the farming districts. It was in demand for knitting stockings, winding wire hat frames, embroidering, and, of course, for cloth. In this period, prior to the introduction of the power loom in America, the farm market would provide a good output for yarn, if ways could be found to reach this demand that was to extend along the Atlantic seaboard and to some extent inland.

109

Effective marketing is a concomitant of efficient production, and Almy, Brown & Slater became noted for their development of sales methods for which there was no precedent. Slater had demonstrated his ability to produce superior cotton yarn. That was his job, and it was the job of Moses Brown to sell it. Here was where shrewd Moses Brown exhibited his ingenuity, based on his lifetime experience in dealing with dollars and men. How far should he trust agents to whom he had consigned yarn to be sold on commission: these strangers who resided in localities as far north as Portland, Maine, and as far south as Charleston, South Carolina—spots seemingly as distant as the corners of the earth, in his day of limited transportation and communication facilities? How generous a commission should he allow them, without sacrificing all of his profits?

His English competitors were also having difficulties in disposing of their yarn products. A series of business failures in England and Ireland had caused a drop in the market value of the cotton cloth into which their yarn was woven. What better means of disposing of their surplus than to send it to America, even though this country now possessed the Arkwright methods, thanks to Slater? Agents from England came with offers of well-woven cotton cloth at such low prices and such long-time allowances for payment that it was heartbreaking to the American manufacturers, whose embryonic ventures in machine spinning were dependent on the local market for the yarn from which cotton cloth was woven.

A little earlier, when Ireland had flooded the English market with their surplus, the British government had taken measures to regulate the market; then England, regardless of

American manufacturers, began flooding our markets with their unsalable goods. "It is doubtless for the discouragement of the manufacturers here," Moses Brown wrote; and he recommended government regulations of our own comparable to those in England. But Slater's firm continued to make yarn in spite of market conditions.

At the start Almy, Brown & Slater, to whom Almy & Brown were responsible for marketing, depended on the local weavers as customers for the yarn produced. Its first lot of yarn to be sold (June 1791) amounted to one hundred and sixteen pounds, for which they received £35 3s.4d., or about $1.00 a pound. This was disposed of near Providence, mostly, although some was sold as far distant as Norwich, Connecticut. By 1801 small amounts of yarn were being sold to retailers in Portland, Newburyport, Marblehead, New Bedford, Salem, and Boston. With sales to Rhode Island and Connecticut, the aggregate quantity sold was sizable. Large amounts were also sold in New York, Albany, Philadelphia, and Baltimore. Home weaving was greatly increased because of the good machine-spun yarn now available, for as late as 1810 only two per cent of American cloth was made in cotton mills. The mills received the raw cotton and shipped the finished yarn by water, at this stage, although the rapidly extending turnpikes were soon more frequently used for shipments. The delivery of Almy, Brown & Slater's yarn to Norwich, for example, was simple, for it was on one of these new turnpikes on the way to New York. Slater believed so completely in this improvement in transportation as necessary to progress that he is said to have owned $40,000 worth of stock in turnpike companies when not too much stock was available.

As we read their correspondence with their various agents we can well believe that Almy & Brown's own commission of four per cent was far from excessive at this period.

Some five years later, competition with mills that had adopted the Slater processes required Almy, Brown & Slater to reach farther north and south for their markets. Already the new partner, Obadiah, had been sent south to Alexandria, Virginia, and its outlying towns, to introduce the superior Almy, Brown & Slater yarn. Even as far afield as Charleston, South Carolina, they endeavored to drum up a market.

The usual method of the firm was to sell on consignment, with commission on the yarn sold. This was good bait to introduce their yarn of course, for the firm accepted all the risk at times of poor sales. When it felt strong enough, it tried direct selling, but with little success. Their many agents, now well distributed along the Atlantic seaboard, felt more comfortable when Almy, Brown & Slater again assumed the full risk at times of poor sales of yarn.

In a few years, Almy, Brown & Slater had attained a position of business stability that was to stand them in good stead in an impending crisis: that caused by the ill-conceived Embargo Act (1807) and the Non-Intercourse Act (1809), whereby America hoped to keep neutral in the Napoleonic Wars between England and other nations and France.

In England, the sons of Jedediah Strutt were also in difficulties as they sought to extend the market for their yarn and stockings during the Napoleonic Wars.*

---

* See Note 7, Appendix A, p. 188.

The Cotton Market

It was a period of hard times for the young American textile enterprises. Samuel Slater met this situation with characteristic aggressiveness by the start of still another cotton-mill venture that grew into a large textile center under his management.

5

THE TIMING OF the initiation of Slater's next textile venture, at Oxford, proved perfect. Three years after the passage of the Non-Intercourse Act, America declared war with England (1812) because of the impressment of American seamen by the British. The ensuing war-engendered prosperity created a demand for textile goods, and the young American textile industry again became active. A year before the war Slater had begun his investigations of the site of the Oxford cotton mill, and a few months after the declaration of war, Oxford was in operation. As in the case of Slatersville, two factors decided the site of the new mill. It had to be in a farming district (since all farm folk knew the hand processes of spinning and could quickly be trained to the machine methods), and it had to have good water power.

Just across the border line between Rhode Island and Massachusetts were farming villages along a stream with a good flow and rapid current. This was the French River on which local people had built tiny grist and sawmills since colonial days. A tributary of the French River, now called Mill Brook, was the outlet at the northerly end of a large pond, called for generations "the pond with the long name." Few can spell its name, which has an Indian derivation: Chargoggagoggmanchauggagoggchaubunagungamaugg Lake.

Samuel Slater had heard of the water-power possibilities of the French River and the pond which was one of its larger sources. He sent an employee to explore it—Bela Tiffany, one of two brothers, sons of a friend who had persuaded Slater to instruct them in the intricacies of the promising business of machine spinning.

Traveling by rough roads that later became the Providence and Douglass Turnpike and the Gore Turnpike, a distance of some thirty-five miles, Bela Tiffany reached the pond and began his explorations. He proved to be a young man of good judgment, capable of appraising the water-power flow and head, as well as the value of the small mills then in operation. He also considered the expenses of building the larger mill required for spinning.

Bela found that Elijah Pratt owned the most promising site. It was in Oxford South Gore, at the outlet of the long pond. It had a "Grist-mill, with two run of Stones, tolerably good; a very good Sawmill; and a Trip-hammer shop, in good repair," per his letter to Slater. His letter called it, however, "the most benighted part of the Globe, 4 miles from Oxford, 3 from Dudley, 6-1/2 from Thompson." Slater, of course, got the significance of this last comment. It meant that he must include in his investment the cost of land and new dwellings for mill hands, near the mill. They could not travel such long distances to and from work, before sunrise and after sundown, over the wretched roads.

We may skip the various negotiations whereby Samuel Slater soon had purchased, in Bela's name, the superb Pratt water-power site and, in the Slater manner, had bought (by 1812) many acres of adjacent farms and various flowage rights, so that there could be no dispute as to who owned the right to utilize this water power.

Late in 1812, Bela Tiffany sold five-sixths of these properties to Samuel Slater; a legal technicality which would make Slater the recorded owner of the property. The other sixth was probably a commission for transacting the business or to give him partnership status, since there is evidence that later Samuel bought out Tiffany's interest to dissolve a partnership formed at this time called Slater & Tiffany. The water power was developed and a "modern" cotton factory was built. It was called the Green Mill, and began spinning cotton yarn in the next year.

This accomplishment had been carried out during the expanding activities of three other mills which required Slater's guidance.

A more poignant trial at this time to a man of Slater's keen sensitivity was the loss of his wife Hannah.

Hannah Slater died on the day of her twenty-first wedding anniversary, October 2, 1812, in her thirty-eighth year. The epitaph that Slater erected reveals his estimate of her character and gives a measure of his loss. We may read this today, on the weathered horizontal slab in the Slater family plot in Pawtucket:

> To distinguished endowments of nature
> Were added acquirements
> Which endeared her to all acquaintances
> And fitted her to perform with honor and fidelity
> The various duties of domestic life.
> Her benevolence was warm and gracious
> And in her the poor and distressed found
> A consoling friend and generous benefactor.

Slater was left with a family of six boys, ranging in age from three weeks to ten years. As has been noted, the Slaters had already lost three children; and Samuel Jr. had been born in 1802. George Bassett was born February 12, 1804; John (probably named for Samuel's brother) May 23, 1805; Horatio Nelson (who went by the name of Nelson) March 5, 1808; William (named, as so often happened, after the first-born who had died) October 15, 1809; and it was Thomas Graham who was the little baby when his mother died; he was born September 19, 1812. So, in addition to all Slater's business problems which because of the uncertainty of the times demanded much of his attention, he was once more faced with personal loss and with the necessity of solving the seemingly insoluble problem of finding a housekeeper to take the place of a mother to the boys.

The development of his new mill at Oxford South Gore was most urgent, to take advantage of the demand for textile products caused by the War of 1812. This mill approached more nearly to being a complete cotton mill when Slater constructed a dyehouse and buildings for bleaching. John Tyson, an experienced dyer, was given an interest in the business and came from Pawtucket in February 1812 to arrange the machinery and start dyeing. Soon the yarn from the Green Mill was being dyed on the site, and a little later carts or chaises brought yarn from the Old Mill and the White Mill in Pawtucket to be dyed. Soon a company store was built for the convenience of the mill hands and the profit of the mill owners.

By cutting off our foreign commerce for several years, the War of 1812 caused many cotton and woolen mills to be erected, making America independent of Great Britain for its calico and broadcloth. When the war ended it had been a time of great rejoicing—loud salutes from parks of cannon, sham battles, parades of army and naval veterans. Then came the sober aftermath, particularly for the cotton industry. With the end of the war came another flood of English cotton goods on the American markets. These imported goods were usually in the form of finished cloth made from machine-spun yarn, which had been either hand-woven in England or woven on Cartwright power looms, then coming into operation. They were sold or consigned at ruinous prices with which the American cotton mills could not compete. The New England cotton mills had produced large quantities of yarn during the war. All had not prospered, because of the extravagant wartime costs of their construction and their poor management. Certain statistics indicate that before the war ended there had been 65,000 spindles in operation, of which the largest quantity in one mill was at Slatersville: 5,170. By 1816 only a few spindles were turning.

Two factors overcame this depression in the cotton industry, upon which so many cotton growers, mill hands, and mill owners depended for a livelihood. The Protective Tariff Act was passed on April 27, 1816, to protect American capitalists and workers. It called for specific, minimum, and ad valorem taxes, the latter ranging from $7\frac{1}{2}$ per cent to 30 per cent. The whole tariff system was now remodeled. The minimum feature was introduced for the first time and was applied to cotton cloths of a certain description, and on cotton twist, yarn, and thread. This was the first tariff adopted as a protective

118

act. The vote in the House was 88 to 54; in the Senate, 25 to 7.

The other factor was the introduction in America of the power loom that had now been perfected in Great Britain. About two years earlier, a start in American power weaving had been made in a small mill located at Waltham, Massachusetts. Its founder was Francis Cabot Lowell, who with associates later built the textile city of Lowell, Massachusetts, and shared with Slater the credit for the development of the cotton industry during the ensuing decades. With the protective tariff and the power loom the American textile industry regained its position and continued to expand.

At this time Bela Tiffany sold the rest of his interests in the Oxford South Gore business to Samuel Slater, who already had further plans for its expansion; ultimately it was to embrace sections of the towns of Oxford and Dudley. These areas were incorporated as the town of Webster, several years later.

The impact of Samuel Slater on the town of Webster, Massachusetts, is best described by quoting an estimate of his character, written forty-two years after his death, when Webster was approaching its heyday as a great American textile center. At this time a contemporary historian of the town thus describes Samuel Slater:

> Mr. Samuel Slater made this town his residence many years, and died here on the 20th of April, 1835, aged 67. No man of his time engaged in business in this country was more generally known or maintained more highly his integrity for fair and honorable dealings,

or whose moral worth was more highly regarded. His naturally kind feelings inclined him to acts of benevolence, and no one with a just claim for favor left him without partaking of his liberality . . . the rise and progress of this business [Samuel Slater & Sons] has made the town of Webster . . . .

IV
Father and Sons
1817-1829

1

HANNAH SLATER HAD been dead five years, and with the cares of his expanding business activities, Samuel Slater had had to solve the problems of bringing up his six boys. They were in the care of a Negro housekeeper who was not always kind to them. Before the War of 1812, Samuel had made an English friend, Robert Parkinson, who, with his wife, Esther Parkinson, lived in Philadelphia. He was a buyer of American cotton that was now becoming an important source of supply for the English cotton mills. During visits of the Parkinsons to Pawtucket, Hannah and Esther had become close friends. The John Slater family had also enjoyed the Parkinson visits. When Robert Parkinson died, Slater assisted his widow in settling her husband's estate.

On September 23, 1817, Samuel wrote "on a momentous subject," to Mrs. Robert Parkinson, widow, Philadelphia.

> Dear Madam,
> As the wise disposer of all events has seen fit in his wisdom to place you and me in a single state—notwithstanding, I presume none of his decrees have gone forth which compels either of us to remain in a state of widowhood. Therefore, under these and other circumstances, I now take the liberty to address you on a momentous subject. I have been inclined for some time

past to change my situation in life, and have at times named you to my brother and sister for a partner, who have invariably recommended you as suitable and have fully acquiesced with my ideas on the subject. Now if you are under no obligation to anyone, and on weighing the subject fully, you should think that you can spend the remainder of your days with me, I hope you will not feel reluctant, in writing me soon to that effect. You need not be abashed, in any degree, to express your mind on this business, for I trust years taught me to receive your reply favorably, if my understanding has not. I have six sons to comfort you with the oldest is about fifteen years, he has been at Oxford about a year, (not Oxford in Great Britain), the youngest is in his sixth year, I believe they are all compos mentis, and they are as active as any six boys, although they are mine. Cousin Mary is now down from Ludlow on a visit; she has a noble corpulent son about six months old. I should have divulged my intentions to you months past had not my brother given me to understand that he expected you daily on this way to visit. Probably you may consider me rather blunt in this business, I hope you will attribute that to the country that gave me birth. I consider myself a plain candid Englishman, and hope and trust, you will be candid enough to write me a short answer, at least whether it be in the affirmative or negative, and should it be in the negative, I stand ready and willing to render you all the advice and assistance in my power relative to settling your worldly matters.

With due respect, as a friend and countryman, I am, dear madam, your well wisher,

Samuel Slater

N.B.—Hope you are a freemason as respects keeping secrets.

The Children

Two months later, Samuel Slater and Esther Parkinson were married in Philadelphia by the Reverend Joseph Pilmore, Rector of St. Paul's Church. The new Mrs. Slater came to the home in Pawtucket that Slater had built eighteen years earlier, and met his six boys.

An important factor in the business success of Samuel Slater was his remarkable ability in the selection of associates to help him carry on the ever growing Slater interests. His happy choice of a second wife was similarly fortunate when it came to the bringing up of his young sons, and in his social relationships as well. That the boys took to this charming woman is evident from his frequent, jocose remark: "You have stolen the love of my children from me."

Their proper education was now the important problem. Shortly, we shall see that the education of the Slater sons was to be of a twofold character—simultaneously with their textbook schooling there was to be a rigid training in the solution of the problems involved in the construction and operation of cotton mills.

In the business phase of their education they were under an able teacher whose confidence in the ability of his boys in their early teens to accept the heavy responsibility he assigned was rewarded by their success under his kindly yet strict guidance.

It is possible that he conceived the idea of a textile estate to be called Samuel Slater & Sons during this period of the education of the boys. This would indicate that he was confident that they had inherited from him the same qualities he had inherited from his own father, and from their mother's forebears a good measure of the Wilkinson talent. But there must be first the boys' preparation for college.

In the spring of 1818, Samuel Slater and his wife, Esther, set out on a ninety-mile trip by chaise, to explore the merits of The Episcopal Academy of Connecticut at Cheshire, a few miles north of New Haven. This institution served as a college, theological seminary, and boarding school. They had taken with them not one of the older sons, but little Nelson, who was only ten.

The Connecticut River had to be crossed by ferry, and the ferryman poled his boat to the shore, at the loud blast of the ferry horn blown by Slater. The Slaters, horse and chaise, were ferried across and then taken by the ferryman to a nearby tavern, where they were to spend the night. When it came time for supper, they met their ferryman again, now serving as innkeeper. He was carving a fine roast, which the three enjoyed after their long, chilly ride. Whether husband and wife took part in the dance that followed, when the table and chairs were cleared away, is not recorded. In the morning they continued their long journey to Cheshire.

Arriving there they made arrangements for the Slater boys to attend the school, and the horse was harnessed for the return trip home. Esther climbed in and then Samuel took the driver's seat as the light chaise adjusted itself to his heavy weight. Apparently the Slaters planned to leave Nelson at the school, although they had not warned him, for when he set foot on the step he was told that they had to leave without him; he was to stay at Cheshire. He was told that his brothers would come soon to keep him company, and there would, in fact, be a vacation for him soon. Whether the child protested

126

at this notice that he was to be left among strangers at the school, while his father and mother went home, is not recorded. Our guess is that he took things in his stride, this son who was to survive his older brothers and to carry on and expand Samuel Slater & Sons, for decades thereafter.

Nelson got his vacation, and returned with George to Cheshire after Easter in 1818. Samuel Jr., who was frail, did not go at this time.

Samuel Slater gave the two boys stern instructions to write home every fortnight, and George, who was fourteen, did so with reasonable faithfulness. The letters of ten-year-old Nelson were not frequent, and a standard closing of George's was: "Nelson wishes to be remembered by you all." Samuel Slater would chuckle at a naïve letter finally received from Nelson: "I attempt to address a few lines to you, hoping, that you will consider they are written by a little boy and therefore will not be disposed to view them with a critical eye." The father considered the ability to write well-composed letters to be very necessary in business affairs, and he would appreciate this grammatically precise one from Nelson. Letter writing was not easy for young or old, in the year 1818—one from George to his brother John bore the postcript: "NB excuse my writing for my [goose quill] pen was poor and I had not a suitable knife to mend it."

There were other boys from Pawtucket and Providence at Cheshire, and a Mr. P. Minor and his wife, who were friends of the Slaters, kept an eye on the sons, helping them to buy clothes and in other matters. Best of all, Minor's father had a farm in Middletown, where he would take them on holidays to hunt and fish. Their studies came first, however, as a glance at some of their letters will prove.

Soon, Nelson was studying Latin and making good progress; also he was learning Greek, algebra, arithmetic, and English. Both he and George found English composition their most difficult subject. They spoke on the stage every other Wednesday, at which time they read their compositions; and attended church every Sabbath. One letter expresses their appreciation of the cake that Mr. Tiffany had brought from home. Their attire was an important matter: boots, stocking yarn, shirts, and cloth for a greatcoat are mentioned in the letters.

Meanwhile John, who was fifteen, was at Oxford, tending to his father's activities there. A letter from Slater to son John promises him a new hat, and in a postcript admonishes him to "be obliging, steady, industrious, and pleasing and do not forget Reading Writing & Arithmetic. Do think of these acquirements and practice them while young." The practical John replied with two letters, the first mentioning his need of stockings and clothes for summer, and the second including a business-like statement of the affairs at Oxford. Several hands were removing a portion of the bleach house and were finding that large stones were making hard digging for the foundation of the new store that was to adjoin the bleach house. It was however, a better site than the one previously contemplated, which was in sand and often wet sand at that, the boy wrote.

Samuel Jr. was soon to join his brothers in Cheshire, although his increasing suffering from tuberculosis would soon require him to return to the Pawtucket home. He was now eighteen, and his father would miss his eldest son's help in the operation of the two Pawtucket mills while the boy was at school. He had been particularly helpful during Samuel Slater's recovery from a serious accident which had confined him to his home for several weeks.

In young Samuel's first letter from Cheshire to his father he inquired whether it was eighty-three or eighty-six dollars his father had given him. His father's reply was that he had counted it twice and had made it eighty-six dollars the first time and eighty-three the second, and ended by hoping that "you will be a good boy and endeavor to learn all you can." In this letter, an interesting item of news told that a cousin of the Slater boys had been to New Bedford and signed up for a whaling voyage of two to three years.

The father had asked young Samuel for an account of his expenses on his trip from Pawtucket to Cheshire. Samuel replied that stage fare from Providence to Norwich was $8.00; steamboat fare from Norwich to New Haven $14.40, and stage from New Haven to Cheshire $3.86. In this letter, as in all the correspondence from the Slater boys to their father, love to all the family was sent by young Samuel.

In September of 1820, he had to return home; his disease had become very serious, and a letter from George states his fear that his older brother will not recover if he does not become more prudent in the matter of exposing himself, in such matters as riding "into Providence several times for a month past . . ."

Now the time had come for son John, who was fifteen, to stop his practical education in the cotton business for a while, and to attend Cheshire. Nelson was the only Slater there, for George had enrolled at Brown University in Providence. Just how long the father could spare the practical John from business activities appears a question, as we read their correspondence.

In reply to John's concern at the poor health of Samuel Jr., the father says that the brother was "but little if any better." He adds a short admonition to be passed along to Nelson: "Do tell Nelson that if he expects to stay much longer at Cheshire he must write me once in two or three weeks. I do not feel satisfied with his neglect." A later letter to John says, "They are going on pretty well at Oxford . . . They want your assistance there." He was glad to realize that Nelson had realized "that he at length could muster up courage to write me a letter, hope he will write again soon." Nelson was growing up; he was now twelve.

Describing the new activities at Oxford, in response to John's request for information, Slater wrote: "I fear your services will be wanted up there before your year is out at Cheshire . . . you will not fail to improve every moment of your time in order to be the more useful in business when you return."

Throughout this correspondence between father and sons in the spring of 1821 runs a growing anxiety about the health of Samuel Jr. When the end came, in July, the father wrote John telling him of the death of his oldest brother. He described the son's last days and his funeral—". . . some say there were about 100 carriages. . . ." This last statement provides a measure of the respect in which the people of Providence and Pawtucket held Samuel Slater and his family.

The letters between father and sons, and from brother to brother, were written in the formal diction of a century and a half ago. Their formal language does not obscure the deep family affection that existed. The loss of his eldest son, of whom he had expected so much in his future plans, affected Slater deeply. He beseeched the others to care for their own health; his love for them was amplified by a determination that they be prepared to take over the estate he was creating for their future prosperity. This is revealed in a letter to John, just then the most experienced in the business.

Another letter to John, written shortly before young Samuel's death, would indicate that the father was beginning to feel his age, for he wrote:

It is highly important that one or more of my sons was learning the business so as to, in some measure, relieve me from the close attention which I have to attend to —

In great haste,
Your affecte. Father
Saml. Slater

2

AMONG THE PROFUSELY decorated homes of Pawtucket notables exhibited during the great Cotton Centennial of the year 1890 was a large two-story brick house, which was then seventy-one years old. The front of its cupola was mounted with three American flags; other flags draped the iron railings of the portico roof, and red-white-and-blue buntings, with still more flags, adorned the facade of the house which faced Pleasant Street. This house drew more attention than any other during the celebration, for it was the Slater Mansion—once the home of the man whose achievements the Cotton Centennial commemorated. His wife, Esther Parkinson Slater, had built it in the year 1819.

Esther was a wealthy woman in her own right. Learning that Hezekiah Howe had been unable to complete his new house at the foot of Church Hill in Pawtucket, she had purchased it for the sum of $6,500, and finished it. The Slater family then moved in, and son George, now sixteen, wrote, "I am glad to hear that you are all well. I suppose by this time you are well settled in your new brick house. It may be that you now wonder how anybody can live in a wooden house. . . . "

The Slater family enjoyed living in this commodious dwelling; yet, as it turned out, it was not to be their only home.

132

There was soon another one constructed for the family. In that day of limited travel facilities, a man with Slater's widely distributed activities required more than one house to live in.

With the mill at Slatersville making good progress under the management of his brother John, Samuel realized that his own attention could be best concentrated on the Slater Oxford development. Too much of his own time was spent in travel from Pawtucket by chaise, carriage, or in a chilly sleigh over the long roads, which were dusty, muddy, or paved with ice, according to the season (today the trip would be a matter of an hour or so, by automobile) so he bought an old wooden house that straddled the Oxford-Dudley line and lived there between weekend trips. He remodeled this old New England farmhouse into a brick house, and he wrote his son John that he would be interested to know that it was expected that "the roof is on the new brick house by this time." There were the usual moving difficulties that occur when one is to live alternately in two places. We may read his letter to John, dated July 13, 1822, to realize this situation. The letter is worth quoting; it reveals how the busy Samuel Slater had to come down to the everyday facts of life in family affairs.

Oxford July 13th, 1822

Dear Son
John Slater
I send the bearer, Caleb Dunham, down to Pawtucket, in order to get some money, etc., etc., by whom you will send up 4 or 500 hundred dollars, also my flannel shirt, 2 or 3 loaves of sugar out of the box upstairs & a dozn. of good lemons. 2 pieces of sacking out of the Side Board, 2 patch work bed quilts with the pieces to finish it—All the Cotton Carpetting you can find,

133

leaving enough for the boys bed rooms—Nancy can find the keys of the Side Board, in the middle drawer of the Beauro—Send up all the important letters that have come to hand & inform me how you get along at the Old Factory — . . . ."

In haste, Your respectful Father
Saml. Slater

The story of the career of Samuel Slater now enters a wider scope. Up to now, it has been sufficient to treat of the achievements of the man himself. Henceforth, we find ourselves describing the activities not merely of Samuel Slater, but of his family as well. Although still in their 'teens, the Slater sons were growing up, and the family correspondence reveals more and more of their business activities.

George, now the eldest son, had come to help his father in Oxford. There were no Slater boys at Cheshire; most of them lived at the brick house in Pawtucket. The plan was to have Nelson, now fourteen, go to the Oxford Mill and learn how to spin good Slater yarn.

By the middle of 1822, John was so much needed in Oxford, and his father in family affairs at Pawtucket, that they changed places; Samuel resided in Pawtucket, but for the next four years, John divided his time between the Slater mills at Pawtucket, Providence, Slatersville, and Oxford.

The Slater activities at Oxford included the production of hand-woven cotton cloth, utilizing the weaving talents of the wives and daughters of farmers and mechanics of both nearby and distant villages. The yarn was consigned to country merchants, each of whom would distribute it over a tract of from

134

six to ten miles from his store to be woven. For taking the yarn and returning it in the form of cloth, a weaver was paid four cents per running yard for plain cloth that was three-quarters of a yard wide. Plaids of the same width brought eight cents; and bedticks ten cents, if three-quarters of a yard wide. This arrangement continued from 1812 to 1823. It was popular with the womenfolk—they could earn cash to buy the tempting products of the merchants' stores. Even with the coming of the power loom, some time was to elapse before hand weaving was wholly superseded by machines.

Early in his Oxford activities, Samuel Slater had made the acquaintance of a fellow countryman named Edward Howard, who was skilled in the processing of woolen yarn and cloth. As was his wont with men from England, Slater had befriended Howard. The latter is credited with being the originator of the manufacture of woolen cloth in Oxford, in a mill that started operation in 1814. Its broadcloth was probably the first to be made in America. This mill burned down in 1822, but a new one had already been started on the French River, and began manufacture under the firm name of Slater & Howard.

Bela Tiffany, John Tyson, and Edward Howard were the pioneer managers who executed the plans of Samuel Slater that started Webster on the way to prosperity. Tiffany, who had left the firm in 1816, was highly regarded by his senior partner, Slater. Tyson, who died in 1821, was held in particular esteem by Slater because of his integrity and ability in the management of the Oxford Dye Works. Howard was called the "Jolly Yorkshire-man" and was big and convivial, but Slater found him to be a man of far from admirable traits of character, despite his ability to make good wool products.

The association of Slater with Howard was a rare instance of his selection of a partner who proved lacking in integrity and business judgment. Howard remained a Slater partner for fifteen years. Then matters came to a head in 1826, and Samuel turned to his son John, then twenty-one, to straighten things out. Extracts from his letters to John reveal the situation. "It will be necessary to put a clerk into S&H's store . . . to see that no property whatever is delivered out on Mr. H's private demands." . . . "I think it would be highly advisable for you to go over and take possession of every note that is payed to S&H." . . . "Consult Counsell as often as necessary." . . . "I wish to turn them into cash in order to meet the demands against S&H." . . . "I have got to pay in Boston this next March about Forty Thousand dollars & the Lord only knows where it is to be got. Money remains very scarce yet, & how I shall get along with that dirty fellow's contracts, time alone must unfold." Samuel Slater had trusted a rascally partner, and had to bear the loss.

Early in January 1829, Edward Howard sold his undivided half of the property of the Woolen Manufacturing Company to Samuel Slater and his sons: George B., John, and Horatio Nelson. It was the beginning of Samuel Slater & Sons. George was twenty-five, John twenty-four, and Nelson twenty-one.

That Howard's mismanagement had hurt the reputation of the woolen mill, and that of its senior partner as well, is indicated by Samuel Slater's announced determination to restore it to "respectability." A month after the withdrawal of Howard, Slater wrote:

> Samuel Slater & Sons have come to the determination
> to place that ignoble establishment in Dudley, called
> "Slater & Howard's Woolen Factory," in a state of
> respectability. Whether or not it was got up in iniquity,
> I cannot say; but I fear some things during the life of
> it are mysterious. It is the united wish of S. Slater &
> Sons to sink into oblivion the past inroads that have
> been made, one way or another, on that establishment.
> They are very anxious to place the business in future
> on a fair mutual ground, so as to save about six thou-
> sand dollars a year for extra stock, raising the wind,
> bad debts, and too liberal commissions . . .

The firm of Slater & Howard was reorganized under the
name of the Dudley Manufacturing Company and continued
in existence until after the death of Slater.

For several years, the three elder Slater sons had received
their dual education: that attained from textbooks and the
practical training taught by a master instructor, their father.
They would now continue to work under his directions, but
with an added incentive—their decisions must be made in the
knowledge that as limited partners, their own money was at
stake. (Within a few years, the father was to die, bequeathing
his entire textile estate to these three sons.)

The Oxford property of Samuel Slater & Sons included all
the water-power rights on the French River and the pond, the
cotton and woolen mills there, the pond itself, and the large
real estate holdings which Samuel had acquired since his start
in Oxford in the year 1812. It encompassed the portions of
Oxford and Dudley that in 1832 became the town of Webster, so named because of Slater's admiration of Daniel Webster.

A schedule of Slater's estate in 1817 will serve to show the progress of his business:

> I own the house &., in which I live in Pawtucket, one other house, and six house lots, one house and land in Seekonk, and third part of the old factory, so called, counting fifteen hundred spindles, water priveleges, stores, and five dwelling houses; and one third part of three farms in Attleborough and Saybrook. One house and lots near Hartford, also one quarter part of several buildings and lots in Providence. One quarter of a brick house in Boston one quarter of the estate in Smithfield, containing two cotton factories, with between five and six thousand spindles, together with three water priveleges, about thirty-five good houses and twelve hundred acres of land. My estate in Oxford, Mass., consisting of one cotton factory of two thousand spindles, one woollen establishment, grist and saw mill, sixteen dwelling houses and seven hundred acres of land. Also one handsome farm in Pelham, and a right in six mortgaged estates, to the amount of ten thousand dollars, which I shall have to hold.

It is easy to believe a biographer who says Slater often quoted an English proverb: "He did not keep more cats than caught mice." From his report it would seem that the Slater cats were good mousers.

The extensive acquisition of farm lands and other real estate by Samuel Slater during the seventeen years that had elapsed since his start at Oxford is evidence of his confidence in his own ability to create a large textile establishment in the area and the enhanced value of the entire locality that should result. Quoting a sage historian, "He [Slater] foresaw that a rapid advance in population would follow: consequently as rapid an advance in the surrounding lands; furthermore, it enabled him to control the principal affairs of the place, and to prevent any intrusion upon his plans." Such complete control of an American town would appear undesirable today. In the paternalistic period of the time of Samuel Slater it was sufficient, and Webster continued to prosper for years. Today at Webster there is a large stone house built by Slater for his son George and now occupied by his descendants. It is a museum of relics of things used by Samuel Slater during his life. Among these are graceful chairs of Colonial pattern; andirons made by Oziel Wilkinson, with turned globes on the standards, supported by splayed feet; silverware; a Deed Book of the Slater land takings that is still consulted in land settlement disputes; and the trunk used by emigrant Slater on his voyage to America.

Rats have eaten most of the rawhide binding of the wooden trunk. On one portion, however, the leather still remains, held by the tacks that spell S S, the initials of the owner. It is a small trunk, 27" x 14" x 11-1/2" in dimensions, with thin iron straps and well-secured angle irons at corners.

Samuel Slater was unfortunate in that neither of his two younger sons, William and Thomas Graham, ever attained partnership caliber. In William's case, he died nine years before the firm of Samuel Slater & Sons was started. William was a sturdy youngster who became a cripple as the result of a serious accident at the age of thirteen. A favorite stunt was to "tread the water wheel" at the Oxford Mill when the clutch was disengaged—a most dangerous, boyish trick. William caught his foot between a wheel bucket and bulkhead, and it had to be amputated. He would not accept an artificial foot, and became a husky boy, despite his stumpy foot. His handicap, however, seemed to have affected his attitude toward life. Several times he tried to run away from home. After one unhappy runaway trip to Honesbury, Pennsylvania, his father arranged for William to take a proper trip, under suitable guidance. It was to be a voyage to Savannah, Georgia, no less; then to continue to England, France, and the East Indies. This fine trip ended at Savannah, when William died of yellow fever there in 1826, at the age of sixteen years and eleven months.

As for Thomas Graham, it appears that his father had made a mistake, at least in Thomas's case, when he had arranged for a legacy of eight hundred dollars a year for each of his sons when they reached the age of twenty-one. Up to the date of his maturity, Thomas had a good record, and it was reported to his father that he was very useful in the Oxford store, where he bought and sold goods and made invoices. Two weeks later, after Thomas had received his legacy, his father wrote John: "Where is Thomas? Has he rec'd his legcy? If so, how much of it has he already squandered away?" Thomas played the horses, and was not always successful. Two months before his death, Slater wrote to John: "Enclosed is Thos. G. Slater's note to A. Bates which I hope you will settle, as I had much rather have him paid than those horse-jockeys in Southbridge, Sturbridge, & elsewhere."

To the end, his father or his brothers had to pay the debts of the happy-go-lucky Thomas to keep him out of jail. He died nine years after the death of the father who had tried so hard to straighten out this wayward son.

140

3

DURING THE DEPRESSION in the cotton industry, following the War of 1812, Samuel Slater learned of a tiny cotton mill in New Hampshire that had been forced to close because of the American market's being flooded with British goods at prices with which the American textile industry could not compete. It was reputed to be at a water-power site of splendid possibilities, and with his wife and son Nelson, Slater drove by chaise to investigate. He was so greatly impressed with its advantages that he provided funds for the resumption of activities in the mill. A few years later, under his active management, the now prosperous development became the Amoskeag Manufacturing Company, which after his death became internationally known as having more spindles than any other textile plant throughout the world.

The story of the start of Amoskeag provides a typical example of the accelerating growth of the still small cotton industry in America. Men with ambition, energy, and courage would make the start. Running into difficulties because of their lack of knowledge of the novel processes, some of them failed to succeed until experienced men such as Slater took charge.

In the year 1804, a carpenter named Benjamin Pritchard heard from the Indians of the great falls on the Merrimack River a few miles upstream from his carpenter shop. On horseback along the trail to this favorite Indian fishing ground, he rode to the site and found that Jonas Harvey already had a sawmill there. When Jonas learned that his visitor wished to start a cotton mill, he sold or gave him water-power privileges, and even helped Pritchard build the mill. Perhaps he was glad to have a neighbor in this lonesome place: Goffstown (later a part of Manchester) was on the west bank of the Merrimack River, sixteen miles from Concord, New Hampshire, and twelve from Amherst. A few months later, however, Jonas sold his sawmill to Capt. Ephraim Stevens and went back to farming. Next, Pritchard and Stevens, with his brother Robert, reached an agreement to "keep in good repair the milldam at Amoskeag Falls." There would be water enough to drive not only the sawmill, but a cornmill and one for cotton and woolen manufacture as well. The two Stevens brothers were to receive five dollars each, annually.

Their wooden wing dam was actually only a half-dam. It extended from the west bank to a large rock in the middle of the river; this was the local custom, for water-power rights only went to midstream. Power came from an old-fashioned "undershot" waterwheel.

At the start, the enterprise was practically a failure—the mill was poorly built, the second-hand machines inadequate, and the help inexperienced in the machine spinning of yarn. However, when the Stevens brothers put up two thousand dollars, and with the war market for yarn, the mill prospered until the end of the War of 1812. It then closed up shop. In 1822 it was sold out to Olney Robinson, to whom Samuel Slater furnished the money to pay the required price: about five thousand dollars. Robinson proved to be a poor businessman; his energy and enthusiasm was not sufficient to keep the little mill in operation. Slater was forced to foreclose and take over, in about 1825, with five other partners.

When Slater took charge, there were the original mill and a partly built one that he soon completed, and with the true Slater touch, named the Bell Mill because it had a bell to tell the help when to go to work. Later, still another mill was built: the Island Mill built on a midstream ledge.

Slater replaced the old spinning frames with frames that he knew would work. He added what was as much an innovation to himself almost as to his partners: "a few power looms." It had taken some time for Slater to adopt these. From the age of fourteen, he had known how to spin good yarn by machine; his conservatism would not let him accept the power loom until his brother John had persuaded him to do so at Slatersville. There the machines were successful and simplified matters greatly.

Previously, a mill agent had been recognized along the country roads by his enveloping mass of skeins of yarn, piled high on the saddle of his horse, in front of and behind him. His yarn load would lessen as he parceled it out to the weavers in the farmhouses he passed, but it would be replaced by the woven cloth, handed him by those who had finished weaving his last yarn assignment and now wanted pay for the cloth they had woven. It took much bookkeeping to keep straight the yarn *out* and the woven cloth *back*.

All appreciated the power loom, except the home hand-weavers, who now had lost their jobs unless they would be willing to accept a less skilled position in the new cotton mills.

143

Tiny Amoskeag Village, together with a small part of Goffs-town, prospered greatly, as the mills prospered. They employed about a hundred families, perhaps five times that number of persons, when it is realized that father, mother, and children worked. They were happy, according to the standards of a century ago. They toiled in the mills six days a week, from the peal of the mill-bell at six-thirty A.M. until it pealed again at seven-thirty P.M.; and they had a half-hour lunch period at noon. These were the days when mill hands worked seventy-five hours a week. Since there was little money, yarn became the common currency and their wages were paid with yarn.

Indicating that the American cotton industry had begun to reach toward maturity, the six Amoskeag partners sought ways to expand their prosperous development. In the year 1831 they began to acquire all the land on each side of the Merrimack River for a mile above and below the mills, including all the water-power rights as far north as Concord. They soon owned over four square miles of property. Such investments required much money, and to get it they incorporated in that year, with a capital stock of the then tremendous amount of one million dollars. Samuel Slater changed from a partner to a stockholder, and continued so until the time of his death.

Shortly after his death, developments on the east bank of the river were started, and by the time the little wooden mills on the west bank in Amoskeag Village had all burned down, the great development of Amoskeag on the east bank in Manchester had been started. For one hundred years Amoskeag was recognized throughout the civilized world as a great American textile enterprise.

144

4

Two other cotton-mill developments were added to the Slater interests during the period he was putting the Amoskeag venture on its feet. The first was the Jewett City Cotton Manufacturing Company in Connecticut. The second was the Providence Steam Cotton Company—the first steam-powered textile plant in Rhode Island, as well as one of the first in America. Both ventures were family affairs with the Slaters: Samuel and his brother John and the sons of each having shares in their construction and operation.

At an early date, Eleazer Jewett had erected a combined gristmill, sawmill, and fulling mill, at the junction of the Patchaug and Quinnebaug Rivers, in Connecticut, near the Rhode Island border. In the year 1809, a cotton mill was started a little upstream which later became the Jewett City Cotton Manufacturing Company. It had been allowed to run down, and soon Samuel and John Slater bought the mill for seventeen thousand dollars. A letter from Samuel to his son John asks him to send fifteen hundred dollars toward making the down payment. The mill was put in good working condition; a new dam twenty feet in height was built, and the business was conducted as a partnership under the name of S. & J. Slater.

145

John Slater had seen Samuel's sons become proficient and wished one of his own boys to learn the business too, and in the rejuvenated Jewett City mill, which prospered, he saw an opportunity to train one of his sons in the management of cotton mills. From time to time he suggested that Samuel sell his half interest to him. In 1831 this transfer was made, and now the sole owner, John placed his sixteen-year-old son, John Fox Slater, in charge.

That there had been a misunderstanding between the two brothers as to the terms of the transfer is evident in the post-cript of a letter from Samuel to his own son John, then traveling in England:

> N.B. I have this day closed the business with your Uncle John relative to my moiety in the Jewett City concern, he has (though not fairly) taken the advantage of me. . . .

Pawtucket, Slatersville, Oxford, Amoskeag, and Jewett City each possessed what was then the prime requisite for a proper site for a cotton mill: adequate water power. In America, Samuel Slater and his competitors had, perforce, located their cotton mills along rivers. A river had to be selected which had a reasonably adequate flow throughout the year, with its bed and banks so naturally constructed that sturdy dams could be erected and still leave ample pondage areas above them.

The deep roar of the water flowing over the dam's spillway was a potent indication of the power that the river was contributing, via the flume, to the mill's success. Slater was merely following the practice of the English textile men. They used the one source of energy sufficient to drive the many textile machines which the muscles of men in the little home handicraft shops could not begin to operate. Even with her great cities teeming with idle laborers, England had had to build her cotton mills in the rural areas, where labor was comparatively scarce, but where there was water power. This situation had continued for several years, until the Scotsman James Watt had so perfected his steam engine that it could be depended upon, after which steam-powered textile mills had become common in England and later in the United States.

Unlike water power, steam was unlimited in its scope—a mill owner merely had to enlarge his boiler plant and install more engines, when more textile machines were added. Naturally, Samuel Slater wished to test the advantages of steam for American cotton mills, and in the year 1827 he did so.

In the city of Providence, which had a large population of laboring men, anxious for work, the Slater family erected one of the first cotton mills in America to use steam instead of water for power. It was designed with seven thousand spindles, and also important, power looms were used, thus avoiding the problems presented by the use of hand looms; a difficulty which had heretofore kept the Slater mills from being integrated—for all processes—under one roof, as modern mills are constructed.

Its incorporators were John Slater, 2nd, George B., Horatio Nelson, and two others, with Samuel Slater furnishing part of the capital. Within two years he had taken over complete control.

Of course the new mill was called the Steam Cotton Mill— then constituting good advertising to let the public know that its proprietors were alert to promising new processes. Today, when one sees a steam laundry, steam box factory, or any

147

other factory bearing the word "steam" in its title, he may be sure that it is very old, dating back to the era of Samuel Slater, when steam power was a novelty.

As has been noted, a typical Slater characteristic was his wise selection of men and his habit of rewarding those who lived up to his expectations. One such case was that of Thomas J. Hill who, at the age of eight, had started to work for Slater at the Old Mill in 1813. With his experience there, at the White Mill, and other Slater locations, he had become a good machinist, growing up with the development of textile machinery, now so improved that it was a far cry from that which Slater had built in Pawtucket so many years before. Slater's watchful eye had noted Hill's progress and in 1834 he "graduated" him from the two-room machine shop in the steam mill to become a partner in a new Slater enterprise called the Providence Machine Co.

The business formula by which Samuel Slater carried on his many ventures was not in the form of a single corporation, constantly expanding in size as new units were added. Slater worked in partnerships, and by the end of the year 1828 had been a member of thirteen partnerships. Except for his first, Almy, Brown & Slater, he had taken the lead in the organization of these partnerships. Only two had been dissolved: one, Samuel Slater & Co., by the sale of his share in the White Mill to the Wilkinsons in 1810, and the other, Slater & Tiffany, by his purchase of Bela Tiffany's interest at Oxford in 1816.

The following is a list of the thirteen partnership firms with the date of organization of each:

1790   Almy, Brown & Slater   Pawtucket, R. I.
1801   S. Slater & Co.   Rehoboth, Mass.

1806	Almy, Brown & Slaters	Smithfield, R. I.
1812	Slater & Tiffany	So. Oxford, Mass.
1813	Oxford Dye-house Co.	So. Oxford, Mass.
1814	Slater & Howard	So. Oxford, Mass.
1817	Providence Iron Foundry	Providence, R. I.
1817	Springfield Manufacturing Co.	Ludlow, Mass.
1823	S. & J. Slater	Jewett City, Conn.
1826	Amoskeag Mills	Manchester, N. H.
1827	Providence Steam Cotton Co.	Providence, R. I.
1827	Slater, Wardwell & Co.	Providence, R. I.
1827	Slater & Kimball	So. Oxford, Mass.

V
The Textile Industry
1829-1835

1

By 1829 SAMUEL SLATER was at the peak of his career. Prosperous cotton mills, either under his complete control or in which he had large interests, were in successful operation in Rhode Island, Massachusetts, Connecticut, and New Hampshire. In forty years the young English immigrant, whose only asset was his knowledge of the Arkwright methods of spinning cotton, had become an outstanding industrialist, whose name was the symbol of success in the now thriving cotton industry in America. Nearly one-half of the total amount of cotton used in the world was now grown in America. Although much was exported, Slater's New England mills as well as those of other sections in America provided a substantial market for American cotton. Not only had Slater acquired wealth, but due to the technical knowledge he had taught them, had contributed to the prosperity of many others, whether mill owners or hands. Now, at this time of flood tide he was to encounter financial reverses which for a time threatened to ruin the great Slater estate.

The cycle of textile activity had again made full swing. The universal distress that came immediately after the War of 1812 had been succeeded by a period of prosperity, but in 1829 a slump in trade of even worse severity occurred. Because the textile industry had grown substantially larger, the distress was correspondingly greater than in the years 1815 and 1816 when the earlier depression had occurred. Immediately before the 1829 debacle Slater's manufacturing enterprises were in a sound position. Total indebtedness was very limited; payrolls were readily met by the proceeds from the sale of the goods produced. Slater also had many thousands of dollars invested in real estate, secured by mortgages.

Normally, he would have been in a good position to ride safely through this period when the solvency of textile property was highly suspect because of the drop in demand for its products, just as he had gone through the depression of 1815-16 successfully. He found himself greatly embarrassed, however, by his responsibility for the debts of his brothers-in-law, Abraham, Isaac, and David Wilkinson, besides others whose notes he had endorsed, who had not been wise enough to restrict their commitments within safe limits. When these men, one by one, suspended payment, the aggregate amount of their debts which Slater was called upon to pay was $300,000, which for that day was a large sum. Stirred by the general advance of American industry, largely influenced by the dramatic success of the recently completed Erie Canal, the textile industry had gone ahead too fast. While Slater had kept his own expansion within bounds, he became the victim of his tendency to endorse the ventures of talented younger men, of whose honesty and potential business ability he was confident.

A glance at Slater's correspondence will reveal the seriousness of his situation and his spirit of determination through this period of adversity.

154

January 7th, 1829:

. . . It is rather a pinching time here for money . . . since the failure of Hurd [woolen manufacturers of Lowell] . . . almost everyone who has seen or at least touched a cotton or woolen factory . . . are afraid that I have a very heavy load on my back . . . as it respects the Amoskeague and steam cotton manufacturing company, including the woolen factory and all my private concerns (which I consider very trivial), I think I can boldly say, after the whole company debts are paid (all of which I have to meet), there will be left from $800,000 to 1,000,000 dollars, to all concerned . . . .

June 15th, 1829:

. . . . a dreadful storm in and about Pawtucket . . . on Friday last Samuel B. Harris made an assignment of his property without even consulting his endorsers, A. & I. W. On Saturday A. & I. W. made an assignment of their property . . . as soon as the alarm was given in Providence the Providence people, with their lawyers and sheriffs, were busy enough until midnight on Saturday night . . . but too late . . . .

July 29th, 1829:

. . . . Since I wrote you D. W. [David Wilkinson] has gone down the falls. His failure is a serious one, and it affects my mind and body seriously, and purse too for the present, but hope eventually to meet with but little loss.

August 3rd, 1829:

. . . In regard to my endorsements for D. Wilkinson, they are heavy without doubt, but I am secured for the whole eventually . . . As I have to look up entire new friends to aid me in my unexpected liabilities, makes my task more arduous . . . As respects to your observations relative to your fears not being unreasonable, I make every allowance, after taking into view your informant, whom I for years have thought was a *near-ox,* but now I have reason to believe the *off-side* is more congenial to his feelings . . . When I see any of you face to face I will give you a history of *human* or *inhuman* generosity.

Two of my consignees have already offered to loan me $10,000 each, over and above the amount of invoices, whom I have not been acquainted with *"forty years"* . . . .

Sentiment did not deter Slater from taking steps to meet his obligations. Three years earlier, he had written his son John that the balance due him on the last three years from his Slatersville interest was much less than that from his interest in the Old Slater Mill. "On the whole the Old Factory is worth noticing, though old and decrepit like myself," his letter had concluded. He loved the Old Mill, but now he sold his one-third interest in it to William Almy and William Jenkins for fifteen thousand dollars to obtain money toward paying his debts.

As a result of his heavy endorsement of the Wilkinson notes, Slater was forced to take over their mills at Wilkinsonville, a part of Sutton, Massachusetts. These mills were reorganized when he took control and incorporated the next year as The Sutton Manufacturing Company (1830). He also took over the Providence Steam Cotton Mill, which had been built three years earlier, financed largely with Samuel Slater funds.

To William Almy he sold also the Slater one-fourth interest in the Almy, Brown & Slaters mills at Slatersville. Four years later, having bought back his interest in these mills, Samuel

156

Slater with his brother John bought out the interest of Almy & Brown, and the property remained in the hands of the Slater families for many years.

There was grave concern among the businessmen of Rhode Island when Samuel Slater announced how he proposed to solve the problem of paying the debts for which his endorsement had made him responsible, with his only assets the many textile plants on his hands which could only be sold at a fraction of their value. He was determined, as a last resort, to close all the Slater mills and wait out the depression, gradually selling the properties held by him as security for the notes he had endorsed.

It would be bitter medicine—bitter to Slater, for it would mean distress to faithful factory executives who were friends that had helped him; bitter to local merchants whose prosperity depended on the large Slater payroll throughout the State; and bitter to the capitalists who had financed the merchants and who would suffer when the trade of the mill hands ceased. It was probably because it would have been such a bitter pill all around that people awoke to the realization of how tremendously essential Samuel Slater was to the well-being of the community, and they forced the capitalistic investors to sit down with Slater in an attempt to devise ways and means to keep the mills in operation.

The result was that in August Slater executed a deed of trust whereby for $250,000 nine Providence men, as trustees, would hold all his property for a specific purpose. In return, they would advance him money totaling $215,000, secured by his notes. If Slater succeeded in paying the notes as they became due the deed of trust was to become null and void. Otherwise they would sell his mills to recoup the notes.

It was a mutual gamble, with both parties winning if the textile depression should end within a reasonable time, as they felt it was bound to do, because of the necessity for yarn and fabric to clothe the people of the rapidly growing young American nation. With the cash secured by the thirty notes, Samuel Slater could pay the debts of his Wilkinson relatives and resume his normal business of operating and expanding his cotton mills.

It soon became evident that he had not only saved the Slater estate, but re-established his position as an outstanding leader in the textile industry of New England, which again became prosperous.

The spirit of Samuel Slater, exhibited as he weathered the gale in 1829, reveals strong traits of character not called upon during his previous career. He was not used to being in debt beyond his ability to pay. As we review his steps to solve his difficulties, we have to admire the buoyant spirit of this man, who was past sixty. He was not a well man, subject to physical ailments that the over-straining of his physical and mental energy had subjected him to—a man to die within a very few years because of these ailments.

Throughout the struggle he was supremely confident of his ability to come out unscathed—financially, that is. He suffered, however, from the defections of friends of the period of prosperity, and showed a natural bitterness caused by the desertion of friends whose esteem had come from favors granted by him when matters were going well. Throughout he kept his sense of humor, albeit a humor that exhibited a sadness at the lack of stability in fair-weather friendships, specifically that of one of his first partners, William Almy. Almy is presumed to be the "offside-ox" mentioned in one of the letters that have been quoted.

He met this transitory upset in American industrial progress with his typical philosophy. He would not allow anything to stop him in a venture he knew was sound: that of the textile estate of Samuel Slater.

2

In November 1831, a man wrote enthusiastically to a friend about the proprietor of an extensive textile center, a location that was to become the town of Webster a few months later:

> . . . He [Slater] is now in his 64th year. His benevolence and philanthropy have been coextensive with his means; and few have done more to bring young and enterprising men into business than Samuel Slater. He has, probably, now a larger amount employed in manufactures than any single individual in the United States. The firm here is Samuel Slater & Sons. They have 7 mills, 2 of stone, 3 of brick, and 2 of wood. Five of these derive their power from French River; the other 2 are in the center of the village and obtain their power from Slater's lake. . . .

It was evident that Samuel Slater was not only back on his feet; he was in a stronger position than ever.

It was a good time for a textile establishment to be in a strong position, ready to take advantage of the surging growth of America, which had increased its population by one-third during the previous decade. An important factor was that means for the transportation of yarn and fabric to supply the clothing for the growing populace were expanding. Stirred

160

by the success of the Erie Canal, promoters in other sections were building other waterways to transport men and goods. At this time, five of today's great American railroads made their start, now that it had been proved that steam locomotives could successfully operate on iron tracks. It was the very year in which Cyrus McCormick constructed his first reaper that was to revolutionize the agricultural industry of America.

Fate did not allow the senior partner of the firm of Samuel Slater & Sons to develop its activities to an extent commensurate with the high spirit of industrial advance of this period. It was the sons of the firm who had to keep pace with the growth of American industry.

By the mortality standards of the day, Samual Slater was an old man. Although mentally he was at his peak, physically he was not strong. He is quoted as saying that he had labored sixteen hours a day, for twenty years successively, and he might have added, in the most laborious of occupations. The splendid physique with which nature had endowed him had been impaired by these years of overwork, and too, he did not always take the necessary precautions normal to his age. Intent on his objective, he would step briskly without regard to obstacles in the way. There is the scanty record of a severe accident in 1818 that kept him in his bed for several months; and of his falling through loose boards in a new factory floor that apparently only Samuel Slater could inspect. He was confined to his home for some time thereafter because of the severe bruises that came from this accident.

The worries of solving his financial difficulties during the panic of 1829 were supplemented by severe physical ailments. Some of the letters to his family written during this time made mention of his stomach distress, of his emaciated knee, his rheumatism. What seemed to him to be a cheerful note was added in one by his saying he could make out to hobble about his room two or three times a day, on crutches.

Probably in no better way are personalities and characteristics revealed than through personal letters, written with no thought of future publication. Samuel Slater's are excellent examples, with a quaintness in phrasing and an underlying humor which make them of particular interest. The following one, addressed to "Messrs George B. & John Slater," was written at North Providence, February 8th, 1832:

> Dear Sons, — I wrote John on the 28th ult. that I thought it would be advisable for one of you to come down and see your sick brother, hoping it might in some degree revive his drooping spirits since which time have decidedly not heard from either of you, only circuitously, that you were in Boston. I hope your brother Nelson is rather more comfortable. . . Probably the presence of one of you might make his journey out there rather more aggreeable. As the Rev. J. Fletcher once wrote to his friend who had omitted writing for some time, he asks, "Are you alive, paralytic, gouty, slothful, or too busy to write a line to your friend?"

> Your affectionate father,
> Samuel Slater.

Esther Slater was a tower of strength to him at such times, and his letters written to her in these years reveal much of Slater's kindness and consideration, his concern about the welfare of the various members of the family, and the steps he took to insure their comfort and convenience in spite of his many activities and personal discomfort. The length of detail as he describes his work shows how completely Esther was taken into his confidence, a state of affairs which was not common in those days:

Mrs Samuel Slater, Pawtucket R.I.

Webster, February 25th, 1833

Dear Wife,

I left Wilkinsonville the same day which you left there sick. Son Nelson informed me that your health was measureably improved. Indeed I was, in some degree, satisfied that the salubrious air of Pawtucket would soon reanimate you. I have been tolerably well since I arrived here until a few days past. On Thursday last I traveled round on foot to view some house lots, in the snow broth, and got my feet a little damp, if not perfectly wet. The night following was very cold and froze very hard. The next morning after *breakfast*, not in the afternoon, I recommenced my pursuits, and as I was much older and more clumsy than I thought I really was, that while I was going up a steep frozen hill, and being not sure-footed, I happened, accidentally, to fall prostrate on the ice, to the annoyance of my hip and shoulder. I am now some better, but am severely afflicted with a cold, probably partly from sleeping alone. Last Wednesday morning, about 5 o'clock, a little granddaughter came to town: she and her mother (as the old woman's sayings are) are as well as can be expected. Son John arrived here last Saturday night, and, no doubt, before this time has kissed the baby, &c. &c.

I shall endeavor to leave here as soon as the sleighing will permit. . . .

A certain hook which has been baited with shiners, for some time past, will not induce a certain mackeral

163

to bite, or at least to swallow the bait. Further particulars when I see you.

Respectfully yours, &c.
Samuel Slater.

N.B. . . . If Wm Bliss should want a few dollars, towards cutting wood, you will let him have some.

Returning to Pawtucket he became seriously ill. Sons George and John rushed in a chaise forty miles to Pawtucket in response to a letter from Nelson. "Father is very low indeed," Nelson wrote. Slater rallied from this attack, however, and was soon as busy as ever in the business of his mills, his family problems, and the conduct of his farm at Webster.

No one reading Samuel's letter to Esther written from Webster, September 28th, 1833, would know that he was approaching death. It was a buoyant epistle, addressed to the one upon whom he most depended. He talked in the active terms of life, as felt by a man who expected to live forever:

Mrs. Esther Slater, Pawtucket R.I.
Favoured by Miss M. Turner.
Webster, September 28th, 1833
Dear Wife,—The bearer, Miss Mary Turner, would have gone down to Pawtucket, some days past, had I not deferred it on account of seeing my son Thomas, who promised, on Tuesday last, since which time I have not seen and scarcely heard from him, excepting by way of a teamster or tin peddler, verbally. Mrs Turner expects to recruit you up in the course of a week or ten days, and then bring you up into the county of Worcester, where you can see, among other curiosities, a noble stone dam, built after the architectual skill of Sir C. Wren. It is a very heavy job, and you may rely on it, I pay good attention to it. I

164

generally eat my breakfast in season so that I get over there by sunrise, and remain, either sitting or standing on rocks or stones, until sunset; and then during the night I sleep from two to six hours. I enjoy tolerable good health, and my limbs are daily gaining their wonted activity, &c. You will endeavor to find some employment for my new driver, Silvester Davy, during his stay in Pawtucket. If you should come up shortly, I wish you to send a little good West India, which I want for *medicine*. I should like to hear how you and all your invalids get along. I would say many things, but having about forty eye servants under pay, on outdoor jobs, all whom I find it necessary to watch as close as a cat does a mouse, therefore, I must close.

With due respect, &c. &c. Samuel Slater.
N.B. It is a general time of health here.

This was, of course, a brief surcease between a short period of apparent recovery and the resumption of the disabilities that would result in his death about two years later.

Strangers would note the interest of the elderly man, basking in the sun as he watched spans of horses drag huge stones to within the area of reach of timber derricks. They would watch the derrick swing the stones to the crest of the dam, after which the descending tackle would lower them to a position where men could guide them to a precise level and line, to form a permanent structure. The stone dam should serve Samuel Slater better than his earlier wooden ones.

Construction jobs were always of interest, the strangers would observe. They would wonder only at the intense scrutiny of the elderly man, as he watched this activity, and at why this interest would continue from dawn to sunset. The "about forty eye servants," as he described his employees to Esther, would know. Physically decrepit as he was, their boss would see that he should get what he was paying for. So they built him a fine dam in short order.

A flattering event occurred during this period of Slater's illness. This was no less than a visit of President Andrew Jackson, near the start of his second term in the spring of 1833. One might say that Samuel Slater was used to presidential visits, for after the War of 1812, President James Monroe had paid him a visit and Slater had taken him to the Old Mill. Slater had shown Monroe the first frames on which he had spun the first cotton yarn in this country made by the Arkwright system.

Jackson, arriving in Pawtucket after receptions at New York and Hartford, was shown a form of prosperity with which he had not been acquainted. To him, a Southerner, prosperity meant fertile fields of tobacco, rice, wheat, flax, indigo, rye, and, of course, cotton. This village of Pawtucket was prosperous because of its busy Slater Mill, which paid wages high enough to enable citizens of the village to live in warm houses, wear good clothing, and have plenty to eat—the measures of a comfortable standard of living for any community. The President was so impressed that he wished to see the man who was responsible for this pleasing condition, and when he learned that Samuel Slater was confined to his home with rheumatism, he, his Vice-President, and members of his cabinet paid Slater a visit. Certain of the traits whereby Slater had achieved industrial success were similar to those that had made Jackson a successful President of the United States. The two elderly men had much in common, and they had a pleasant visit, at the end of which, the President said: "I understand you have taught us how to spin, so as to rival Great

166

Britain in her manufacture; you set all these thousands of spindles to work, which I have been delighted in viewing, and have made so many happy by a lucrative employment."

"Yes sir," said Slater, "I suppose that I gave out the psalm, and they have been singing to the tune ever since."

President Jackson could think of but one title for a man with Slater's amazing record—he greeted him as the "Father of American Manufactures," a gratifying note on which to end a pleasant visit.

During the period of his increasing feebleness, Slater continued to show the traits of character that had guided his business life. Writing from Webster to his old associate, Moses Brown, now past ninety-five, he apologizes for his five-day delay in answering Brown's epistle concerning the failure of a certain Masonic Lodge to pledge bank shares as security for payment of rent. "I should have answered without delay, had not I been deprived of holding my pen, owing to a lame hand and wrist," he explained. He continued: "I have no surplus cash to spend in the law, but still I, for one, consider a part of my duty to my fellow beings to aid and assist in trying to make people to be honest and upright in all their contracts."

Despite their occasional business differences, Slater harbored no grudges, and he concluded with an expression of his esteem for the elderly business associate of many, many years' standing: "Hoping the many years which have passed over your honorable head, still permit you to enjoy your usual state of health and activity."

It is of interest to note that Moses Brown, who appears to have been a semi-invalid, actually outlived Slater, passing away a few days short of his ninety-eighth birthday.

Still at Webster, Slater became more ill. In April it became evident that the end was near. His condition was described in a letter from Nelson to Thomas: "Father is very low indeed; he has now been confined to his bed for about 12 days with a complication of diseases among which are rheumatism, gravel, with considerable fever and latterly with a very sore throat." Samuel Slater died on Monday evening, April 20, 1835.

Among the testimonials of the character of Samuel Slater and of his place in American industrial history, that contained in his obituary in the *Providence Journal* of April 22, 1835, is particularly pertinent, for it expresses the esteem of his contemporaries. It reads:

> In Webster, at 6 o'clock on Monday evening, the 20th inst. Samuel Slater, Esq., aged 66 years, 10 months and 11 days. Mr. Slater had long been one of our most enterprising and respected citizens and was emphatically the father of the cotton manufacturing business of this country. In all the relations of life he maintained a character for probity and integrity seldom equalled. Few could have died whose death would have been more sincerely lamented by his numerous relatives and friends.

It was customary at the time for newspapers to carry what were termed "Short Sketches" of the lives of various people who had made some outstanding achievement. Although now they are considered dated, they did present an over-all picture in their summary of character and personality. The "Short Sketch of the Life of Samuel Slater," which also came out in the *Providence Journal* and from which the following extract is given, is no exception:

168

Such are the outlines of the business life of a man, whose skill and knowledge of detail, in a business which, up to the time of his appearance among us was unknown to this community, were unrivaled, whose commercial views were of the most liberal and enlightened character,—whose energy, perseverance, and untiring diligence, aided in his early efforts by the money and countenance of those who justly appreciated his merits and confidently anticipated his eminence, have triumphed over obstacles which would have discouraged others; have given a new direction to the industry of his adopted country; and have opened a new and boundless field to its enterprise. It has rarely fallen to the lot of any single individual to be made an instrument, under Providence, of so much and such widely diffused benefit to his fellow-men, as this man has conferred upon them, without any pretension to high-wrought philanthropy, in the ordinary, unostentatious pursuit of that profession to which he had been educated, as a means of honest and creditable living. Yet, unpretending as he was, and noiseless in that sublimated charity, which is now so fashionable and predominant, his sympathy for the distressed, and his kindness and good will for all, were ever warm, active, practical, and efficient sentiments; based upon steadfast principles, and aiming at the greatest attainable measure of good. In the relief of immediate and pressing want he was prompt and liberal. In the measures which he adopted for its prevention in the future, he evinced paternal feeling and judicious forecast. Employment and liberal pay to the able-bodied promoted regularity and cheerfulness in the house, and drove the wolf from its door. "Direct charity," he has been heard to say, "places its recipient under a sense of obligation which trenches upon that independent spirit that all should maintain. It breaks his pride, and he soon learns to beg and eat the bread of idleness without a blush. But employ and pay him, and he receives and enjoys, with honest pride, that which he knows he has earned, and could have received for the same amount of labour from any other employer." It would be well for all communities if such views, on the subject of pauperism, were generally adopted and carried into practice. It is hardly necessary to state, concerning one who has done so much business and with so great success, that his business habits and morals were of the highest character. The punctual performance of every engagement, in its true spirit and meaning, was, with him, a point of honour, from which no consideration of temporary or prospective advantage would induce him to depart; from which no sacrifice of money or feeling were sufficient to deter him. There was a method and arrangement in his transactions by which every thing was duly, and at the proper time attended to. Nothing was hurried from its proper place, nothing was postponed beyond its proper time. It was thus that transactions the most varied, intricate and extensive, deeply affecting and affected by, the general business of three adjoining states, and extending their influence to thousands of individuals, proceeded from their first inception to their final consummation, with an order, a regularity and certainty, truly admirable and instructive. The master's mind was equally present and apparent in every thing; from the imposing mass of the total to the most minute particular of its component parts.

Rising above a hilltop section in a Webster cemetery is a massive obelisk cut from one granite stone of a beautiful texture. It marks the grave of Samuel Slater. It is in the center of the Slater lot, reserved by him when he donated the spacious adjacent acres to the town of Webster for a cemetery. The Slater obelisk is some twenty feet in height, so heavy that three yokes of oxen were required to cart it from the Quincy quarry where it was cut. It is of interest to note that this quarry was engaged at the time in furnishing the many stones needed to build a larger obelisk—the Bunker Hill Monument.

Throughout his life, Samuel Slater had kept strong his religious faith. That it sustained him to the end is evident from a small piece of paper, which Esther found in his Bible, a few days before his death, on which he had written:

> Psalms, chap. XLII, 11th verse—Why art thou cast down, O my soul, and why art thou disquieted within me? Hope thou in God, for I shall yet praise him who is the health of my countenance and my God.

> Prov. chap XVII, 28th verse—Even a fool when he holdeth his peace is counted wise, and he that shutteth his lips is esteemed.

3

THROUGHOUT THE NEAR half century of the development of his great textile estate, Samuel Slater displayed a versatility of talent that was tremendous in its scope. His ingenuity in the design of improvements to the crude early spinning apparatus revealed a mechanical aptitude that was impressive. Although not usually considered an inventor, he designed devices that were of such utility that they were pirated by former employees when they started textile ventures of their own.

Mitchell Wilson, in his *American Science and Invention,* writes:

> He was the first to set up a system of manufacture in which the successive steps of the skilled artisan were broken down into such simple components that a group of children could outproduce the finest craftsman. It was the one system ideally suited to a country that was to be plagued by a shortage of manpower for another seventy-five years. No one saw any discrepancy between such a system and the American goal of enhancing the dignity and human value of the individual. The American factory fed, clothed and equipped men for the fight against a hostile universe; and the factory system was actually considered to be a victory for the American creed of freedom.

As a successful operator of cotton mills Slater came to be considered unique, and as at Amoskeag, had shown that he could revive hitherto unsuccessful ventures in the new field of cotton manufacture. An innate financial judgment based on careful prior analysis led him to undertake ventures that proved sound upon their consummation. He did not gamble.

He was an enthusiastic promoter of textile projects, and there is no record of the failure of any such venture sponsored by him. However, these talents—mechanical, inventive, operational, financial, and promotional—do not explain the unique career of Samuel Slater. They were supplemented by personal characteristics that are equally essential to any explanation of his remarkable success. Matching his tremendous confidence in his own ability to accomplish his ends was an innate quality whereby he inspired the necessary confidence in others that he could come through. The most cogent example of this Slater trait was his quick convincing of the shrewd Yankee-Quaker, Moses Brown, that he should finance Slater at the start.

In later life, Slater once told a friend that he had averaged sixteen hours of work a day during his first twenty years in America. We can easily believe this statement. He had to travel from one mill to another by chaise, or in an occasional stagecoach. He had to write all his correspondence by hand with a goose-quill pen; he had to demonstrate personally many of the processes of his mills, they were so new.

Withal, he found time for the other things of life. He was a distinguished lay member of his Episcopal church, a noted philanthropist, a bank president, and the man whom some credit with the starting of the first Sunday School in America; and like most unpretentious men, he derived a keen enjoyment from simple things in life such as his farm.

He could fight when necessary, but without malice, and his keen sense of humor must have cleared the air often at times of stress. He had improved himself by much reading of the best authors in the English language. His perceptions were quick and his observations of mankind very extensive and penetrating. He knew the depth of every person he conversed with; his particular dislike was related to falsehood, deception, and dishonesty: other faults he appeared readily to forgive, these he never passed over without severe censure. It was no wonder that anyone so indefatigable as he was himself should dislike listlessness and idleness. He used to say, "I will try to help those who will try to help themselves; but those who will not, I do not see it my duty; such ought to suffer the consequences of their indolence." This was a fixed principle with him.

His tenderness to animals and everything under his care showed that he was of a merciful disposition.

He was not a man's man, in the sense of active participation in the various masculine avocations. Rather, he was of dignified presence, yet without austerity. The record of his kindly interest in the problems of hundreds of immigrants from his mother country reveals one of the most heartwarming traits of Samuel Slater.

His will, written almost exactly one year before his death, reveals his shrewd appraisal of the future prosperity of the firm of Samuel Slater & Sons, provided it were left in good hands. It allowed but a limited competence for his son Thomas, to whom the bequest of a large inheritance would not have been wise. It left annuities to his grandchildren; and to his wife, Esther, the furniture of the house in Pawtucket;

pew No. 4, St. Paul's Church, Pawtucket; and six hundred dollars annually so long as she remained his widow. The will referred to articles of agreement made with her at the time of their wedding, wherein she had given up all right of dower and power of thirds in his estate.

There have been few marriages in which the mutual affection of man and wife exceed that of Samuel and Esther. Yet Samuel Slater left the bulk of his fortune, measured by his textile estate, to the three sons whom he had trained in its management. Since Esther possessed an estate of her own, he knew she would be well provided for during the rest of her life. Slater had spent his life in the development of one of the largest textile properties in America. He had saved it from ruin by shrewd moves during the textile depression of 1829. It was his first love.

At the time of their father's death, George was thirty-one, John thirty, Nelson twenty-seven. These three met brilliantly the arduous demands of management of the widespread estate their father had bequeathed them. John, however, lived only three years after his father's death; George outlived his father by only eight years, and it was left to Nelson to carry on the Slater mills thereafter.

Nelson seems to have inherited the largest share of his father's genius at management, and he lived to a ripe old age, active almost until his death in the year 1888, after nearly forty-five years of responsibility in full charge of the Slater estate. He had supervision over the extensive holdings of the firm in Webster, the Webster Woolen Mill, and the Phoenix Thread Mill, Union Mills, and Sutton Manufacturing Company at Wilkinsonville. Nelson adopted novel methods—the establishment of a sales department, instead of sales through agents, as had heretofore prevailed, and the building and operating of a railroad—the Providence, Webster and Springfield line. He continued to expand the Slater activities, keeping them to the forefront of the rapidly growing textile industry of America.

Nelson rounded out the combined activity of father and son to nearly a full century by the time of his death. Two years later, the great Cotton Centennial of the year 1890 was held in commemoration of the start by his father of America's first successful cotton mill in Carpenter's tiny shop in Pawtucket.

These two, Samuel and Nelson Slater, would highly respect those who have carried on the great industry which they began and gave so much of their lives to maintain. And by the same token, the later generations who have carried on in the fine tradition of their progenitor can be justly proud of their heritage and their relationship to one of the truly great men of his time—Samuel Slater, the man who so deservedly won for himself the name: "Father of American Manufactures."

Appendices

APPENDIX A: SUPPLEMENTARY DATA

Note 1: *The Early Promotion of American Textile Industry.*
The "mercantile" policy of Great Britain, under which it governed its American colonies, was based upon the premise that colonies existed for the benefit of the mother country. Beyond their firewood, meats, and breadstuffs, they must look to her for the necessities of life.

He "would not have the Americans make a hobnail!" Lord Chatham had roared in defense of the Acts of Parliament: the Laws of Trade, Navigation Acts, List of Enumeration, and other irksome means whereby the mother country expected to keep its colonies in the status of agricultural communities. They would thus have to depend on her for their manufactured goods and become good customers instead of hard competitors of the spinners, weavers, and hatmakers, and the workers in the iron forges of England.

It was her handicraft industries that England sought to protect at the start. By the end of the American Revolution, however, the mother country owned an asset of vastly greater value to defend—her factory system, developed during the Industrial Revolution.

Now, having no control over the manufacturing facilities of its former colonies, England depended upon its restrictions on emigration of mechanics and the exporting of models or drawings of the machines that were so essential to American industry. The United States would continue to be industrially poor unless these restrictions could be evaded.

179

Outstanding characters active in the determined effort to promote American manufacture were President Washington, his Secretary of the Treasury, Alexander Hamilton, and the Assistant Secretary of that department, Tench Coxe.

Coxe was an able orator and a prolific writer; by word and pen he preached the necessity of the creation of more and more American industries. Although a review of his publications reveals a wide understanding of many industries, it was in the field of cotton growth and manufacture that his efforts were most successful. Coxe was one of the promoters of "The Pennsylvania Society for the Encouragement of Manufactures, and the Useful Arts," which sponsored the American advertisement of a bonus for the construction of certain textile machines that clinched Slater's decision to go to America.

Coxe was most noted, however, for his efforts to promote the growing of cotton in America. He was called the father of American cotton culture. Prior to the Revolution, cotton culture had advanced from the status of a garden flower to its cultivation for the production by hand of yarn and cloth in considerable quantity. Knowing a little about the merits of the Arkwright machines, Coxe wanted them in America, and of course, wanted sufficient raw cotton to keep these machines busy. His efforts were largely addressed to the five Southern States. He induced Congress (1789) to protect Southern growers by a duty of three cents a pound on foreign cotton.

Twenty-one years later Tench Coxe, who had witnessed a flourishing growth in the field of cotton, made a prediction on its promising future: "COTTON—this raw material, being the *only redundant* [abundant] *one* adapted to the manufacture of cloths for apparel and furniture, produced in the United States, and being most susceptible of labor-saving operations, the cotton branch will probably, nay certainly, become, *very soon* the most considerable of our manufactures." Any review of American industrial progress during the early 1800's will show that this prophecy of Tench Coxe was correct.

180

Note 2. *The Arkwright Equipment.* The series of machines in Slater's first American cotton mill has been analyzed as described below. We may consider them as reproductions of those that Apprentice Slater had to operate.

Flake

Preparing the cotton for the card was not done at the mill, but in homes nearby. The custom then was for women to come to the mill and be given quantities of cotton, called buntings, which they took to their homes to be opened up and cleaned on their flakes. The flake was a sort of rack or frame, three feet square and about three feet high. On top of the frame were tightly strung cords or small ropes forming a network of about ½-inch mesh. Cleaning the cotton was done by willow switches, each about three feet long. From ½ pound to a pound of cotton was laid on the flake at a time; a woman then beat the cotton with two willow switches, one in each hand, shaking it up at the same time until it was light and fluffy. She then stopped to pick out the motes, hulls, or other trash that remained in the cotton, the heavy dirt and seeds generally falling through the ropes onto the floor. After she had finished her bunting, usually between 10 and 20 pounds of cotton, she took it back to the mill, together with the pickings of trash, where it was examined and reweighed.

Breaker Card

The cleaned cotton was fed by hand into the back of the breaker card and emerged at the front by means of the doffer and comb as a thin fleece which was then *rolled into a lap.* The lap may have been formed at the card, but most likely the fleece was delivered into a box and then taken to a lap machine.

Lap Machine

The lap machine was probably of the type used by Arkwright. Arkwright's machine consisted of a table about 20 inches wide, 4 feet long, and 2½ feet high. The top of the table had side or guide rails, and at one end of the table, and between the guide rails, was mounted a roll or drum. The fleece was laid on the table from which it was wound around the drum to form a lap.

Finisher Card

The lap then went to the finisher card. The fleece was unrolled and again carded, but this time it was gathered to pass through a round trumpet to form a sliver which was delivered into a can.

Drawing Frame

Two or more cans from the finisher card were placed at each delivery of the drawing frame. This machine consisted of a tablelike frame, supporting two lines of rolls (probably similar to Arkwright's drawing frame). The slivers passed through the system of rolls where they were attenuated or reduced in size and then united into a single sliver which was delivered into a can at the front of the frame.

Lantern or Can-Roving Frame

After the drawing process, the sliver was further reduced in size to make a thin sliver or roving for the spinning frame. This was done by the roving frame (probably the Lantern Frame), which was similar to the drawing frame, only the rovings, after passing through the rolls where they were considerably attenuated, received a slight twist as they were delivered and coiled into a rotating can. When the can was full, the coils were removed through a side door in the can and deposited in a "skip" which was taken to the bobbin winding-wheel.

Bobbin Winding-Wheel

The bobbin winding-wheel consisted of a frame on which was mounted a large wheel and a horizontal spindle driven by a band or belt from the wheel. An empty bobbin was placed on the spindle, and as the operator turned the wheel by her right hand, the roving from the skip passed through her left hand, which she moved back and forth from one end of the rotating bobbin to the other until the bobbin was filled.

Spinning Frame

From the winding-wheel, the roving bobbins were placed in the creel of the spinning frame. This frame consisted of 24 spindles—12 spindles on each side—and was probably similar to the 48-spindle frame later built by Slater and now in the National Museum in Washington. The rovings passed through the roll system and were attenuated or reduced to the required yarn size, the yarns being wound onto small bobbins by means of throstles or flyers. The yarn was then reeled.

Reel

The reeling was done on a machine equipped with a swift consisting of slats held by arms on a shaft rotatable in bearings at the ends of the machine. The yarns were thus wound into skeins or hanks which were sold to stores who retailed them to weavers for their hand looms.

Note 3. *Darwin's Description.* The English physician and poet, Erasmus Darwin (grandfather of Charles Darwin), was so impressed with the novel machine processes of spinning yarn at the Cromford-Arkwright Mills on the River Derwent that he described them in a poem:

—Where Derwent guides his dusky floods
Through vaulted mountains, and a night of woods,
The nymph Gossypia treads the velvet sod,
And warms with rosy smiles the wat'ry god,
His pond'rous oars to slender spindles turns,
And pours o'er massy wheels his foaming urns,
With playful charms her hoary lover wins,
And wields his trident while the monarch spins.
First, with nice eye, emerging Naiads cull
From leathery pods the vegetable wool:

With wiry teeth *revolving cards* release
The tangled knots, and smooth the ravel'd fleece:
Next moves the *iron hand* with fingers fine,
Combs the wide card, and forms the eternal line;
Slow, with soft lips, the *whirling can* acquires
The tender skeins, and wraps in rising spires;
With quickened pace *successive rollers* move,
And these retain, and those extend the *rove*;
Then fly the spokes, the rapid axles glow,
While slowly circumvolves the labouring wheel below.

Note 4. *The Almy, Brown & Slater Agreement.* The following agreement, made between William Almy and Smith Brown of the one part, and Samuel Slater of the other part, —Witnesseth that the said parties have mutually agreed to be concerned together in, and carry on, the spinning of cotton by water, (of which the said Samuel professes himself a workman, well skilled in all its branches;) upon the following terms, viz:—that the said Almy and Brown, on their part, are to turn in the machinery, which they have already purchased, at the price they cost them, and to furnish materials for the building of two carding machines, viz: —a breaker and a finisher; a drawing and roving frame; and to extend the spinning mills or frames, to one hundred spindles. And the said Samuel, on his part, covenants and engages, to devote his whole time and service, and to exert his skill according to the best of his abilities, and have the same effected in a workmanlike manner, similar to those used in England, for the like purposes. And it is mutually agreed between the said parties, that the said Samuel shall be considered an owner and proprietor in one-half of the machinery aforesaid, and accountable for one half of the expense that hath arisen, or shall arise, from the building, purchasing, or repairing, of the same, but not to sell, or in any manner dispose of any part, or parcel thereof, to any other person or persons, excepting the said Almy and Brown; neither shall any others be entitled to hold any right, interest, or claim,

184

in any part of the said machinery, by virtue of any right which the said Slater shall or may derive from these presents, unless by an agreement, expressed in writing from the said Almy and Brown, first had and obtained—unless the said Slater has punctually paid one half of the cost of the said machinery with interest thereon: nor then, until he has offered the same to the said Almy and Brown in writing upon the lowest terms; that he will sell or dispose of his part of the said machinery to any other person, and instructed the said Almy and Brown, or some others by them appointed, in the full and perfect knowledge of the use of the machinery, and the art of water spinning. And it is further agreed, that the said Samuel, as a full and adequate compensation for his whole time and services, both whilst in constructing and making the machinery, and in conducting and executing the spinning, and preparing to spin upon the same, after every expense arising from the business is defrayed, including the usual commissions of two and one-half per cent. for purchasing of the stock, and four per cent. for disposing of the yarn, shall receive one half of the profits, which shall be ascertained by settlement from time to time, as occasion may require; and the said Almy and Brown the other half—the said Almy and Brown to be employed in the purchasing of stock, and disposing of the yarn. And it is further covenanted, that this indenture shall make void and supersede the former articles of agreement, made between the said Almy and Brown and the said Slater, and that it shall be considered to commence, and the conditions mentioned in it be binding upon the parties, from the beginning of the business; the said Samuel to be at the expense of his own time and board from thence forward. And it is also agreed that if the said Almy and Brown choose to put in apprentices to the business, that they have liberty so to do. The expenses arising from the maintenance of whom, and the advantages derived from their services during the time the said Almy and Brown may think proper to continue them in the business, shall be equally borne and received as is above provided for in

185

the expenses and profits of the business. It is also to be understood, that, whatever is advanced by the said Almy and Brown, either for the said Slater, or to carry on his part of the business, is to be repaid them with interest thereon, for which purpose they are to receive all the yarn that may be made, the one half of which on their own account, and the other half they are to receive and dispose of, on account of the said Slater, the net proceeds of which they are to credit him, towards their advance, and stocking his part of the works, so that the business may go forward.

In witness whereof the parties to these presents have interchangeably set their hands, this fifth day of the fourth month, seventeen hundred and ninety.

> Wm. Almy
> Smith Brown
> Samuel Slater

Witnesses—
Oziel Wilkinson, Abraham Wilkinson

Note 5. *Sargeants Trench.* The waterway from above the upper dam to the Old Slater mill is described in the following rather obscure old account, pertaining to the water-power litigation:

> There is no street which bears the suggestive name of Mill St. (now North Main St.) but a narrow path overshadowed by the western woods, runs to the north parallel to the river. In fact there are two streams, one bears the name of Little River, and is formed by a current that diverges from just above the falls, and flows nearly in the direction of present Sargeants Trench. Indeed, there may be said to be three streams; for there is a depression in which, when the main river is swollen by freshets, a volume of water rushes along the gully, and which, subsequently deepened by human hands becomes the famous trench that afterwards figured so largely in litigation. It is presumed that the latter is the Old Slater Mill trench

186

and Sargeants trench which are in use today. Judge Story, in his opinion given in November 1826, published 1827, states that "The lower dam was built as early as 1718." "About the year 1714, a canal was dug, or an old channel widened and cleared on the western side of the river: beginning at the river above the lower dam and running around the west end thereof, until it emptied into the river, about ten rods below the said dam. It has long been known as Sargeants Trench, and was originally built for the passage of fish up and down the river. But having wholly failed for this purpose, about the year 1730, an anchor mill and dam were built across it by the then proprietor's of the land." "In 1792, another dam (Slater's) was built across the river at a place above the head of the trench, and almost twenty rods above the lower dam; and the mills on the upper dam, as well as those on Sargeants Trench are now supplied with water by proper flumes, etc.; from the pond formed by the upper dam."

Note 6. *Strutt contemporary English Cotton Mill.* William Strutt, a son of Jedediah who was now grown old, was almost a fanatic on fire hazards. He had proved to be an efficient son of his distinguished father and became about as famous in English textile history, particularly because of his fire preventive measures. He had been shocked at the complete destruction by fire of the Albion Flour Mill in London that had occurred only a few years after this famous pioneer-mill had been built. When the Strutt activities had expanded to the extent that its new Calico Mill in Derby, a few miles south of Belper, was to be built, William Strutt built the world's first practically fire-resistant factory. It was a six-story structure with its floors paved with brick or tile. These were laid on brick arches, supported by cast-iron beams resting on cast-iron posts. All it needed to be truly fireproof was the encasement of iron beams and columns in non-flammable tile or concrete, as is done today. Strutt's

187

Calico Mill was under construction in England in the same year that the Old Slater Mill was being built in America.

Note 7. *Strutt difficulties during Napoleonic Wars.* The Strutt firm was now operating under the title of W. G. & J. Strutt, each initial of which was that of a son of the famous Jedediah.

A year before the Embargo Act was passed the Strutt firm had received acknowledgment, from E. Viale of Gibraltar, of three "trunks" containing 180 dozen men's cotton hose, per the *Harmony,* valued at £255 15s 4d.

By evading British and French laws that practically prohibited trade with Europe and elsewhere, the Strutt firm had sent this and other shipments, hoping to expand their market. Accounts were settled with Viale two years later, at a loss to the Strutts of £32 12s 9d. The Strutt firm also had difficulties when seeking to trade with Mr. Thomas Ogier of Charleston, South Carolina.

APPENDIX B:

REVIEW OF ALMY & BROWN ACCOUNTING RECORDS

The Handicaps

The early accounting books of a long-established industry contain data that otherwise might not be available for a study of its history. A review of the various Daybooks of Almy & Brown thus provides valuable supplementary information on the relationship of Slater and Almy & Brown in their joint operation of The Old Slater Mill and also on other Slater ventures in which he utilized their mercantile experience. Let us start with the accounting for The Old Slater Mill. We will note the business handicaps, the wide diversity of items to be accounted for, and how thoroughly Almy & Brown kept track of the business of Almy, Brown & Slater. It will also be of interest to note the prices of things more than a century and a half ago in America.

Among the voluminous Slater documents in the Baker Library at Harvard is a bound book labeled:

ALMY & BROWN'S ACC'T WITH SPINNING MILLS
SETTLED SEPT. 27, 1804*

The first entry is dated August 22, 1793. The 6 by 15-inch Daybook of seventy-three pages thus is a history of the accounting activities during the first decade of operation of the Old Slater Mill, which had started thirty-three days earlier.

The busy counting-room of Almy & Brown had merely started

---

* The settlement was based on the last entry in the Daybook, i.e. Dec. 31, 1803.

a new account, that of Almy, Brown & Slater, for which it bought the stock: cotton and other raw materials. The plural "Spinning Mills" meant that this or succeeding Daybooks would also record Almy & Brown money furnished for other Slater ventures besides the Old Slater Mill.

As we review the first Daybook, we realize the limitations of the working tools of the accounting rooms where business records were kept during the period of the American career of Samuel Slater. Improvements did not keep pace with the unusual advance in manufacturing processes of the time. Decades would elapse before a practical typewriter became available, and suitable carbon paper had not been invented. You wrote your letter with a quill pen and copied it in the Letterbook, also with a quill pen, which required a rigid writing technique.

The American banking system was unsettled, particularly with respect to the various state banks, the drafts and notes on which could be of uncertain value and had to be watched. Most of the time, money was scarce, and one usually paid a bill of sizable amount by a promissory note which could not be cashed for several months. All such matters had to be figured by hand; there were no computing machines.

Postal facilities were limited. It would often seem safer for you to send a letter by a friend who was traveling to the town of delivery. Sometimes you would decide to save money by having your friend post a letter at a post office much nearer the addressed location than your own.

Receipt of raw materials and delivery of the finished product were by sailboat or horse-drawn carts, or occasionally by stagecoach if the load was not too heavy. Of course the roads on which they traveled were abominable, and transportation of goods accordingly very slow.

The dual monetary system—dollars and cents versus pounds, shillings and pence—was another handicap under which the bookkeepers of Almy & Brown had to work. The shilling was the

190

coin in which wages were computed and merchandise priced in the period of the early activities of Samuel Slater in America. Years earlier, the Colony of Virginia had declared that the gold Spanish "piece of eight," which in time became the measure of the American dollar, was worth six English shillings. A shilling was therefore worth sixteen and two-thirds cents, and for easy figuring, 16.7 cents continued for years as the value of the shilling, although its value was to vary markedly in later periods of colonial history.

In the year when Slater came to America (1789), the American system of dollars and cents became the law of the land with the adoption of the Constitution. But folks accustomed to paying for things in pounds, shillings, and pence found it hard to change to dollars and cents, and for a generation or two a dual monetary system prevailed in the counting-rooms of America. Goods were often priced in shillings and paid for in dollars and cents, and in some cases goods continued to be priced and paid for by the old system.

Thus the earlier accounting records of Almy & Brown show amounts in pounds, shillings, and pence. Here is the first entry in the Daybook started a little more than one month after the Old Slater Mill began operations.

Spinning Mills to Almy & Brown

1793			£	s	d
8 mo. 22	To 224# 12 oz Cotton	2/	22	9	6

This meant that, on August 22, 1793, they bought 224 pounds and 12 ounces of cotton for two shillings per pound, the total cost being 22 English pounds, nine shillings, and six pence. Its cost in dollars is revealed in an adjustment item dated October 26, 1795, in which an amount of £1292, 15s and zero d is computed as $4039.00. As 12 pence make a shilling and 20 shillings make a £, this shows that the value of a shilling in Providence at this date was 15.6 cents. So at two shillings per pound the first bale of cotton bought by Almy & Brown cost $70.12.

191

Continuing to the end of 1797 all items are priced in £/s/d, that is in pounds, shillings, and pence. Thereafter they are in $ and ¢. The amount in which Almy, Brown & Slater was in debt to Almy & Brown on this date was 9092/11/5¾, and was carried over as $30,308.58. The value of the shilling at this date was therefore 16.5 cents. From the above we can see that the shilling varied considerably in value according to local conditions at the time of its computation, and accountants had to be alert in this matter.

The use of the shilling as a medium for pricing things died hard. Even when Almy & Brown changed to the dollar system, for some time it used both systems in computing the total value of each item, the right margin of the Daybook having two columns: £/s/d $ ¢

The methods of writing the items of the Daybook and also of correspondence pertaining thereto are of interest. Handmade paper was expensive and such sizes that were available were used: there was no standard letter size. Those we can examine today have no letterheads; the writer's signature, and occasionally the name of the firm he represented, provide a letter's only identification. Brown lines on the sheet show where it was folded for mailing, for there were no envelopes. The address is written on the outside of the folded letter, which sometimes shows a trace of the red sealing wax that kept inquisitive folks from reading what was written within. We see no sign of a postage stamp, the mailing cost occasionally being scrawled in shillings or pence near the address.

One talent required of the bookkeeper of Almy & Brown was the ability to interpret what he read in a just-received letter and to enter descriptions in the Daybook that would be interpretable to others. This was not a simple matter, for writer and reader must put up with the tricks of the quill pen.

The writer had to start by "mending his pen" with a sharp knife suited to this delicate operation. Next he must load the pen with the proper amount of ink—too much or too little ink

192

might produce words hard to decipher. Having once touched paper with pen, writers seem to have found it wise to keep it there, with flourish strokes that usually connected adjacent words, and the reader would have to decide just what word was meant. Rarely could the pen make an "e" without filling the hole. Being small it could look like an "r" or an "i" that the writer had not dotted, and the reader would have to scan the context to decide what to call the word.

Particularly hard for the quill pen was the letter "s" with its many curves. As is true today, the form to use depended on its location in word or sentence. However, in the day of the book-keeper of Almy & Brown there was a third form: "ƒ" made like a lower case "f" with the right side of the horizontal stroke omitted. An item of the Daybook might read: Bellows, ƒmith, meaning a blacksmith's bellows; flaxseed would be flaxƒeed; mill-stone became mill-ƒtone and molasses, molaƒfes. The signature: Messrs. Samuel Slater & Sons, with its seven "S's", often appears as a scrawl made with one happy flourish of the quill pen.

Sad indeed would be the modern businessman if he were suddenly required to operate under the handicaps that have been described. He would raise the price of his product immediately, of course, as he measured the cost of additional hours to be spent by himself and employees to carry on his business. Happily awakening from such a nightmare, he would pay high respect to his great-great grandfather who did so well despite the handicaps of business operations that prevailed during the early years of the United States of America.

ALMY & BROWN DAYBOOKS

Daybook #1

Almy & Brown's Acc't with Spinning Mills shows a continuing and healthy growth of the Old Slater Mill during its first decade of operation. A good measure of this growth is found in a review of the purchases of the mill's major raw material: cotton. It also shows the decreasing cost of cotton as the cotton gin, invented in the year of the start of the Old Mill, made the culture of cotton in the South more and more prolific.

Cotton was bought in tiny quantities at the start. In the months of August and September 1793, seven purchases were made totaling 377#, varying from 9#-4 oz. to 224#-12 oz. each. The latter was listed as "Cotton" and priced at two shillings per pound. The remaining six items were listed as "picked cotton" and priced at two shillings and six pence a pound. The unpicked cotton thus cost 31 cents per pound, picked cotton 39 cents. Other purchases during the first two years show cotton varying from 23 cents to 35 cents per pound, indicating the varying qualities of the "bags" of cotton purchased at this time.

Turning toward the end of the Daybook we find that, on December 19, 1803, Almy & Brown bought for Almy, Brown & Slater eleven bags of "Upland Cotton Wool" totaling 3,602 pounds in weight. This was a far cry from the 377 pounds purchased in the summer of 1793 when the Old Slater Mill started operations. The price per pound was 16½ cents, about one-half of the price prevailing in its first year. Pirated by the growers of cotton in Georgia and adjacent states, the cotton gin of Eli Whitney had made the production of Upland Cotton profitable to the plantations, and of a cleaner quality, satisfactory to the one American cotton mill of any significance—the Old Slater Mill.

The many items of cotton purchases are variously described as "Cotton," "Georgia Cotton," "Bag Cotton," "Fleece," "Bales of Cotton," "Picked Cotton," or "Upland Cotton Wool." Listed items of other stock purchases may be divided into construction costs, operating expenses, company store charges, and occasional wage payments, shortly to be listed in a separate account book.

Construction cost items cover expenses for Slater's continuing improvements of equipment, and the factory rearrangements to accommodate them. To be mentioned are: boards (white pine, yellow pine, and maple), brass hinges, screws, nails, cartage, wire, sheet iron, and bar iron, to list a few. Incidentally, nails are priced by the thousand, not in pounds. Sixteen thousand ten-penny nails cost about $1.00 per thousand, or seven cents a pound; shingle nails, 35 cents per thousand.

Cartage of cotton varies from 20 to 24 cents a trip according to the load and distance carted. A common operating expense item in a later account book is that for the storage of cotton, perhaps indicating a surplus inventory. Another frequent operating expense item is that for candles. With many dim hours at dawn and twilight, this is understandable, and candles cost 10 pence (13 cents) a pound in 1793. Other operating expenses include: "½ doz. Bellows at 18 shillings," a "scale beam," and "1 doz Spectacles at 18/." The latter would be helpful as an overseer inspected yarn in the dim, early morning. The mill required many caldrons (2,500 to 2,900 #) of sea coal for the stoves, at $18.00 per caldron. Minor items include twine, wrapping paper, flat files, and town taxes amounting to $14.16.

Company store items are frequent: salt pork; "100# sugar at $16.00"; one barrel flour $9.00; 121# coffee at 25 cents per #; 209# of cheese at 7 pence, or 9.5 cents per #; 12# of tea at ¾ (presumably £¾) or $2.50 per #; and ½ quintal codfish. A wage item in 1796 reads: "To paid Rebecca Cole . . . for herself and children—work in the Mill 24£, 9s 11d ($81.00)."

On December 31, 1803, Daybook #1 ends with the second settlement of Almy & Brown with Samuel Slater:

Spinning Mills in Acc't Current with Almy & Brown

Dr.			*Cr.*		
1803			1803		
12 Mo 31			12 Mo 31		
To our Acct to)			By Spinning)		
date as rendered)			Mills a/c to)		$163,100.41
on other side)	149,061.61		date)		
To [be] accoun-)			By the Inter-)		
ted for with)			est on $20,903.94)		
Saml Slater the)			the difference)		
other Owner of)	18,031.77		between our)		3,992.97
the Mill for the)			Debit and the)		
ballance in our)			Mills debit)		
settlement with)			12 Mo. 31. 1801)		
him, say —)					
	$167,093.38				$167,093.38

North Providence
9 mo 27, 1804

Errors Excepted per
Almy & Brown

It is to be noted that no settlement had been made since 1792, and that Slater had been emphatic in demanding one for the decade that had elapsed. Much could happen during such an extended period.

Although Daybook #1 would support the two top items in Debit and Credit, we have no record on how the lower two items were computed—that of the amount due Slater and that of the interest differential. Slater's amount was uncertain, else why would it be entered as "say"; and we are wholly at a loss to explain the interest adjustment.

Obviously the settlement was a compromise and we can imagine many arguments during the nine months that elapsed before an agreement was reached.

Daybook #2

A second Daybook, in two parts, was begun by Almy & Brown in 1796. It overlaps Daybook #1 in time. One cover is titled: *"Daybook #2."* The period covered is from 3/19/1796 to 1/7/1797. It lists the debits and occasional credits of mill hands, Dr. or Cr. to Almy & Brown. Typical entries are for the purchase of wood to be delivered to Arnold Benchley (Dr.); cotton cloth and one skein of twist to John Field (Dr.); order on Nathaniel Croade (Store Manager ?) for 12 shillings to Susannah Shuman (Dr.); for "picking 144# 13 oz cotton at 4d and also 28# 15 oz to Rachel Hopkins (Cr.)." Rachel was paid 2/15/6, or $9.16, or about 5½ cents per pound of cotton picked.

Turning the book upside down we read on the back cover: "Daybook for Cotton Yarn—No. 2—1796." Its 23 pages list the yarn and miscellaneous items for which Almy & Brown and a few agents were in debit to Almy, Brown & Slater. Typical items are wicking, stocking yarn of various No's., threads, and twist.

Daybooks #3 and #4

There are third and fourth Almy & Brown accounting books pertaining to the Slater activities, starting in 1799 and 1815, respectively. Book #3 therefore overlaps Daybooks No. 1 and No. 2, which have been described. Just how overlapping items are reflected in the second settlement with Slater in 1803 that appears at the end of Daybook No. 1 is not indicated. Certainly, No. 3 and No. 4 used a more modern system by which the debits and credits of those who dealt with Almy & Brown were recorded.

The items in Book #3 are of the same nature as have been described in Daybooks 1 and 2. "Expenses and horse to Foxboro Furnace to acct. Castings" is a debit of $2.00. Other items include brass, bar lead, charcoal, cheese, flour, corn, potatoes, and butter.

On page 34 a heading: *"New Cotton Mill"* appears. As the date is the year 1800, the New Mill must refer to the White Mill in which Almy & Brown had no interest. This indicates the beginning of Slater's utilization of Almy & Brown as merchants for purchases for his other ventures. The first item for the New Mill was the purchase by Oziel Wilkinson of a copper kettle for $38.67 and payment for 600 bricks at 3/, costing $3.00. Bricks therefore cost 50 cents per 100, and the New Mill was debited $41.67 for these two purchases.

Items for "boarding" in 1801 show that male mill hands were charged $2.00 per week for their board by Almy & Brown.

A sizable item follows, which is intriguing. "To my time for and in the Cotton Mill &c . . . 523 days 7/12 of which at $2.00 per day, $610.17. To ditto from Jan. 1st to date being 156 days 1/2 of which at $2.00 per day, $156.00." This occurred in 1799 and 1800. Whose time is indicated by "my": partner Almy or partner Brown, or Moses Brown himself; and why were these services needed in a mill of which Slater was superintendent? Incidentally the "7/12" of this item shows that a working day was 12 hours.

In 1812 an account labeled Slater & Tiffany appears. By then, accounts were numbered, and Slater & Tiffany's account was #54. On Feb. 10, 1812, Tiffany, or some representative of Slater & Tiffany, was "Paid cash per rect [receipt]" in the amount of $1,100. Cash for $400 soon followed. On March 31, $1,000 was advanced to B. Tiffany per receipt; also B. Greene was given $20.00 to buy screw plates and account #54 was debited by these amounts.

During several months similar debits were entered in Account #54. These expenses, of course, pertained to the Oxford Mill, which started in this period. All told, from Feb. 10, 1812, to September 10, of that year, Account #54 totaled more than $9,000, of which $6,500 was for cash. The balance was for materials having to do with the construction and equipping of the

198

Oxford Mill. Among these items were plank spikes, hogsheads of rum, vise, lathe, anvil, handsaw, lemons, old copper, spinning frame, coke, cast steel, salt fish, various dyes, rice, old brass, mule stand, and carting from Salem.

Book #3 closes with the sizable credit item of $1,608.82 to William Dean, who must have been one of the agents used by Almy & Brown to sell yarn on commission. The commission is shown as 12½ per cent.

Book #4 starts on January 6, 1815. Predominating items are debits or credits to various agents. They are described as Nankeen Thread, Gingham, boxes of Cotton Balls (Black), Twist, Ticking, Leather, Chambray, and Candle Wicking.

This book starts a new Slater & Tiffany account, #70, on February 28, 1815. Like those in Book 3, the items are substantial both in Debits and Credits. Slater & Tiffany are debited for the "Interest on $51,734.07 from January 1, 1814 to Sept. 1, 1816 being 2 years, 8 months $8719.47." In all there are 11 such interest items totaling $13,433.85, the annual rate being a little over 6 per cent. It is obvious that Slater & Tiffany drew heavily on Almy & Brown for funds to build and operate the Oxford Mill during its early years. Still another Slater & Tiffany account, #79, appears on December 13, 1816.

The four Daybooks, sometimes overlapping in time, show Almy & Brown's attempt to keep records of the expenses incurred during the early years of their new and unfamiliar business—the making and selling of yarn.

Their several bookkeepers during the long period covered were accurate in their computations, judging by frequent checks of the amounts, whether expressed in dollars or English pounds. There are rather frequent adjustment items, however, indicating the lack of an adequate system of recording expenses when they occurred.

A common adjustment item was that of interest. At the start all expenditures were met by Almy & Brown, and the cost of money furnished by them was a sizable item. Before long there was the matter of profits of Almy, Brown & Slater to be considered, these accumulating in the coffers of Almy & Brown for nearly eleven years before a division with Slater was agreed upon. The mysterious item of $20,903.94 that appears in the settlement of 1804 seems to be for money furnished solely by Almy & Brown for which they claimed and received a credit of $3,992.97 for interest.

Although Slater's part was to produce cotton yarn, he would also be deeply concerned with the Daybook records. Not only did they show the costs of his raw materials, but would indicate how well or how poorly his yarn was selling. When an apprentice, his only interest had been in the production of good yarn; now he was learning the financial problems of cotton mill operations. He would learn much from the accounting records of his Quaker-Yankee partners and the man who guided them—his friend Moses Brown.

Bibliography

SUBSTANTIAL REFERENCES TO SLATER

Published Matter:

Ammidown, Holmes. *Historical Collections,* I (Histories of Oxford and Webster). New York: Published by the author, 1877.

Bagnall, William R. *Samuel Slater and the Early Development of the Cotton Manufacture in the U. S.* Place and publisher not known, 1890.

Batchelder, Samuel. *Early Progress of the Cotton Manufacture in the U. S.* Boston: Little, Brown & Co., 1863.

Grieve, Robert and Fernald, John P. *The Cotton Centennial.* Providence: J. A. & R. A. Reid, 1891.

Harvard Business School. *Almy, Brown & Slater and the American Industrial Revolution.* Cambridge: President and Fellows of Harvard College, 1952.

Lewton, Frederick L. "Samuel Slater and the Oldest Cotton Machinery in America," *Smithsonian Report for 1936: S. Slater & Sons.* New York, 1936.

Walton, Perry. *The Story of Textiles.* Boston: Compiled and written for John S. Lawrence, 1912.

White, George S. *Memoir of Samuel Slater.* Philadelphia: Published by the author, 1836.

Anonymous. *The Slater Mills at Webster.* Place and publisher not known, 1912.

Not Published:

Genealogies: *Slater & Allied Family Histories.*
 Slater, Tiffany Family Histories.

Lewton, Frederick L. *A Biography of Samuel Slater.*

Tower, Daniel. *History of the Old Slater Mill.* Also various Tower notes.

THE ENGLISH SCENE

Ashton, T. S. *The Industrial Revolution*. London, New York, Toronto: Oxford University Press, 1952.

Baines, Edward. *History of Cotton Manufacture in Great Britain*. London: H. Fisher, R. Fisher & P. Jackson, *circa* 1836.

Bannister, Turpin. "The First Iron-Framed Buildings," *The Architectural Review*, London, 1950.

Besant, Walter. "Fifty Years Ago," *In Factory and Mine* (Chap. XVI). London: Chatto & Windus, 1888.

Blyth, H. E. *Through the Eye of a Needle. Story of the English Sewing Cotton Company*. Place and publisher not known, 1947.

Cheyney, Edward P. *Industrial and Social History of England*. New York: MacMillan Co., 1911.

Fitton, R. S. and Wadsworth, A. P. "Overseas Trade During the Napoleonic Wars," *Records of W. G. & J. Strutt*. Place and publisher not known, 1953.

Glover, Stephen. *History, Gazeteer, and Directory of County of Derby, II*. Derby: Henry Mozley & Son, 1833.

Guest, Richard. *A Compendious History of the Cotton Manufacture*. Manchester, England: Joseph Pratt, 1823.

Hollins. *A Study of Industry*. Place and publisher not known, 1949.

Trevelyan, G. M. *Illustrated English Social History, III* (18th Century). London, New York, Toronto: Longmans, Green & Co., 1951.

Derbyshire Guide. Tourist booklet, 1953.

THE AMERICAN SCENE

Benson and Rippey. *Important Events of the Century*. New York: United States Central Publishing Co., 1878.

Brown, John H., Editor. *Lamb's Textile Industries of the United States*. Boston: James H. Lamb Co., 1911.

Bibliography

Chase, William H. *Five Generations of Loom Builders.* Hopedale, Mass.: Draper Corp., 1950.

Currier, Frederick A. "Stagecoach Days and Stagecoach Ways," *Proceedings of the Fitchburg Historical Society.* Fitchburg: Historical Society, 1897.

Depew, Chauncey M., Editor. "American Cotton," *One Hundred Years of American Commerce,* I, 34. New York: D. O. Hayes & Co., 1895.

Depew, Chauncey M., Editor. "Textile Mills," *One Hundred Years of American Commerce,* II, 72. New York: D. O. Hayes & Co., 1895.

Eaton, Allen H. *Handicrafts of New England.* New York: Harper & Bros., 1949.

Edwards, David F. *Saco-Lowell.* (Pamphlet of the Newcomen Society, American Branch.) New York, 1950.

Faulkner, Harold U. *American Economic History.* New York: Harper & Bros., 1943.

Haley, John W. *The Lower Blackstone River Valley, The Story of Pawtucket, Central Falls, Lincoln, and Cumberland, Rhode Island.* Pawtucket: E. L. Freeman Co., 1936.

Heaton, Herbert. *The Industrial Immigrant in the U. S. (1783-1812).* American Philosophical Society, 1951.

Lovett, Robert W. *The Beverly Cotton Manufactory.* Cambridge: Business Historical Society, Harvard Graduate School of Business, 1952.

Miller, John C. *Origins of the American Revolution.* Boston: Little, Brown & Co., 1943.

Mirsky & Nevins. *The World of Eli Whitney.* Place and publisher not known, 1952.

Navin, Thomas R. *The Whitin Machine Works since 1831.* Cambridge: Harvard University Press, 1950.

Straw, William P. *Amoskeag in New Hampshire.* (Pamphlet of Newcomen Society, American Branch.) New York, 1948.

U. S. Government. *Historical Statistics of the United States, 1789-1945.* Washington, D. C.: U. S. Dept. of Commerce, Bureau of the Census, 1949.

U. S. Government. *History of Wages in the United States from Colonial Times to 1928.* Washington, D. C.: U. S. Dept. of Labor, Bureau of Labor Statistics, 1934.

Ware, Caroline F. *Early New England Cotton Manufacture.* Boston: Houghton Mifflin Co., 1931.

Wood, Frederic J. *The Turnpikes of New England.* Boston: Marshall Jones Co., 1919.

MISCELLANEOUS

Arts and Manufactures of U. S. for the Year 1810. (Cotton: Cultivation, Carding, Spinning, and Machinery.) Place and publisher not known, 1814.

Coxe, Tench (Assistant Secretary of the Treasury). *View of the United States* (Status of U. S. Manufactures including Cotton). Place and publisher not known, 1794.

Dictionary of Merchandise. (Cotton-Wool, London.) Philadelphia: James Humphreys, 1805.

Geier, Frederick V. *The Coming of the Machine Tool Age.* (Pamphlet of the Newcomen Society, American Branch.) New York, 1949.

Gilroy. *History of Silk, Cotton, Linen and Wool.* Place and publisher not known, 1853.

Herbert, Luke. "Water Wheels," *Engineer's and Mechanics Encyclopedia, II.* London: Thomas Kelly, 1840.

McUlluck's Commercial Dictionary, I (Cotton). Place and publisher not known, 1840.

Nicholson. "Water Wheels," *The Operative Mechanic and British Machinist, II.* Place and publisher not known, 1826.

"A Spool of Thread," *Scribner's Magazine, XVI,* 1878.

List of Business Manuscripts in the Baker Library. Harvard Graduate School of Business, Cambridge.